AI and Generati~~ve AI~~

for

E-commerce

Unlocking the E-commerce Data for AI-Driven Insights

Mahesh KS

Preface

The rapid evolution of artificial intelligence (AI) has brought transformative changes to industries worldwide, and e-commerce is no exception. As online shopping continues to grow, businesses are presented with an overwhelming amount of data—from customer interactions and purchase histories to inventory tracking and supply chain dynamics. While this wealth of data holds tremendous potential, it often remains underutilized. This book, *AI and Generative AI for E-commerce: Unlocking E-commerce Data for AI-Driven Insights,* is designed to bridge that gap, providing a practical guide for harnessing the power of AI to unlock valuable insights and drive business innovation.

In recent years, generative AI has emerged as one of the most powerful tools in the AI arsenal. With the ability to analyze vast datasets, generate personalized experiences, and even predict future trends, generative AI is poised to revolutionize the e-commerce landscape. This book explores how AI and generative AI can be applied specifically to e-commerce, offering real-world examples, case studies, and step-by-step approaches to integrating these technologies into your business strategies.

Whether you are a business owner, data scientist, or e-commerce strategist, this book will equip you with the knowledge and tools necessary to make informed decisions and unlock new opportunities. We'll cover everything from foundational AI concepts to advanced generative models, all while focusing on practical applications in the e-commerce space. Our goal is not just to explain the technologies, but to show how they can be used to enhance customer experiences, optimize operations, and ultimately, drive revenue growth.

As you journey through the chapters ahead, you'll discover how to leverage AI to make sense of complex data, automate routine tasks, and craft personalized shopping experiences that are tailored to each customer's needs. In doing so, you'll gain a deeper understanding of how AI can serve as a competitive advantage in the fast-paced, ever-evolving world of e-commerce.

We invite you to explore, learn, and apply the insights shared in this book as you unlock the full potential of your e-commerce data with AI and generative technologies. The future of e-commerce is intelligent, and it starts now.

Table of Contents

1. Introduction to Generative AI and AI in E-Commerce

Generative AI is a field of artificial intelligence focused on creating new content, such as images, text, music, and even code, through algorithms that learn patterns and structures from existing data. These systems are trained using vast datasets, enabling them to generate outputs that resemble the patterns in the data. The goal of generative AI is to mimic the creative processes of humans, offering the potential to automate tasks that were traditionally done manually, including content creation, design, and problem-solving. With advancements in machine learning, particularly deep learning, generative AI is becoming increasingly sophisticated and is now being used across multiple industries.

The following diagram illustrates the functions of Generative Ai and AI in E-Commerce

One of the key areas where generative AI is having a significant impact is in e-commerce. E-commerce businesses rely heavily on creating appealing, personalized shopping experiences for their customers.

Generative AI can assist in this by producing dynamic, personalized product descriptions, images, and recommendations tailored to individual shoppers. For example, AI can generate product images that show items in different settings or from various angles, helping consumers get a better sense of what they're buying. This can lead to higher conversion rates as shoppers feel more informed and confident in their purchases.

Additionally, generative AI can optimize marketing efforts within e-commerce by creating personalized advertisements, email campaigns, and social media posts. AI can analyze customer behavior, preferences, and past purchasing patterns to generate content that is more likely to resonate with each specific shopper. This kind of targeted approach enhances customer engagement and fosters brand loyalty by providing consumers with content that feels relevant to them.

AI is also transforming customer service in e-commerce. Chatbots powered by generative AI can engage with customers in natural, conversational ways, answering questions, guiding them through product selections, and even handling post-purchase support. These chatbots can simulate human-like interactions, providing faster and more efficient service than traditional methods. As a result, customers experience a seamless journey, with their needs addressed quickly and accurately, improving overall satisfaction and reducing the strain on human agents.

Another way that generative AI is being utilized in e-commerce is through supply chain and inventory management. AI systems can predict demand patterns by analyzing historical sales data, market trends, and external factors like weather or holidays. This allows businesses to generate accurate forecasts of which products will be in high demand and when. By understanding these trends, businesses can better manage their inventory levels, reducing overstock or stockouts, and ensuring that the right products are available at the right time.

Overall, the integration of generative AI in e-commerce is revolutionizing the way businesses operate and interact with customers. By automating creative processes, personalizing experiences, and optimizing operations, AI is helping e-commerce companies stay competitive in a rapidly evolving market. As AI technologies continue to improve, the potential for further innovation in the industry is vast, with new applications emerging regularly that enhance both the consumer experience and business efficiency..

Practical Example: Generative AI and AI in E-Commerce

Generative AI has the potential to revolutionize e-commerce by creating personalized customer experiences, automating content creation, and improving product recommendations. In an e-commerce store, AI-driven systems can analyze customer behavior, predict preferences, and generate tailored content like personalized product descriptions, offers, and marketing messages. A practical use case is in an online clothing store where an AI algorithm can suggest products to customers based on their browsing and purchase history, enhancing engagement and increasing the likelihood of purchases.

Sample Data:

The data represents the browsing behavior of users on an e-commerce clothing website:

User ID	Pages Visited	Products Viewed	Previous Purchases	AI-Generated Recommendations	Conversion Rate
U001	3	5	2	Casual Shirt, Jeans	0.40
U002	6	8	1	T-shirt, Sneakers	0.55
U003	4	7	3	Jacket, Sweater	0.30
U004	5	6	0	Dress, Heels	0.60
U005	2	4	4	Hoodies, Joggers	0.35

Output and Results:

1. **AI-Generated Recommendations**: Based on the products viewed and previous purchases, the AI system has recommended items that align with user preferences (e.g., Casual Shirt for U001).

2. **Conversion Rate**: This measures the likelihood of a user making a purchase after receiving AI-generated recommendations. U004 has the highest conversion rate (0.60), indicating that personalized recommendations are effective for them.

Observations:

- Users with more browsing behavior (like U002, who visited 6 pages) have a higher chance of converting (0.55 conversion rate).

- Users who made multiple previous purchases (like U005) have a relatively lower conversion rate, possibly indicating that their preferences are more stable and the recommendations may need refining.

- AI recommendations increase the likelihood of conversion, but the impact varies by user. The more personalized the suggestions are (as seen with U004), the more effective they are at converting into sales.

Decisions from the E-Commerce Perspective:

1. **Refining Recommendations**: More tailored and dynamic recommendations should be offered based on the depth of user engagement and purchase history.

2. **Targeted Marketing**: Users like U002 with high browsing but low purchases may benefit from discounts or offers to increase conversion rates.

3. **Optimizing Product Display**: For users like U003 who have lower conversion rates despite multiple previous purchases, it may be beneficial to adjust the displayed items or offer more personalized promotions (e.g., personalized bundles or loyalty offers).

1.1 Overview of AI and Generative AI in E-Commerce

Artificial Intelligence (AI) is transforming the e-commerce industry by automating processes, enhancing customer experiences, and optimizing business operations. At its core, AI uses algorithms and data to enable machines to learn from experiences and make decisions with minimal human intervention. In e-commerce, this manifests in various ways, from personalized product recommendations to improving inventory management. The integration of AI allows businesses to tailor their offerings to meet the specific needs and preferences of customers, thus enhancing engagement and boosting sales.

Generative AI, a subset of AI, takes it a step further by creating new content, such as product descriptions, images, or even entire marketing campaigns. This technology uses deep learning models to generate content that is highly relevant to users, saving businesses valuable time and resources in content creation. In e-commerce, generative AI is particularly useful for scaling marketing efforts, especially when large catalogs or frequent content updates are required. It can automatically generate variations of product listings, ads, or even social media posts to keep the content fresh and engaging.

AI also plays a pivotal role in customer support by providing virtual assistants and chatbots that can handle a wide range of inquiries, from order tracking to product recommendations. These AI-driven tools are available 24/7 and can resolve common issues instantly, enhancing the customer experience while reducing the burden on human staff. Furthermore, AI chatbots are designed to learn from interactions, becoming more efficient and accurate over time, which helps businesses maintain high levels of customer satisfaction.

In inventory and supply chain management, AI enables businesses to forecast demand more accurately, minimizing the risk of overstocking or running out of products. Machine learning algorithms analyze vast amounts of historical sales data, market trends, and other variables to predict the quantity of goods needed at different times. This allows e-commerce businesses to optimize stock levels, reduce operational costs, and improve overall efficiency in their supply chain, making the shopping experience more reliable for customers.

AI-driven pricing strategies have also gained popularity in e-commerce. By analyzing competitor prices, demand fluctuations, and customer behavior,

AI can dynamically adjust pricing to maximize revenue and sales. This allows businesses to remain competitive while ensuring that products are priced optimally. Additionally, AI can detect trends and market shifts, providing valuable insights that help businesses stay ahead of the competition and make more informed pricing decisions.

Finally, AI is revolutionizing the way e-commerce businesses approach marketing. Through targeted advertising and personalized campaigns, AI can analyze customer data, such as browsing behavior, purchase history, and demographic information, to deliver relevant ads. This level of personalization ensures that marketing efforts are more effective, increasing the likelihood of conversions. By continuously learning from user interactions, AI helps refine marketing strategies and ensures that businesses reach the right audience with the right message at the right time.

Practical Example:

An e-commerce website selling electronic gadgets is looking to improve its product descriptions and advertisements by leveraging Generative AI. The goal is to enhance creativity, appeal to potential customers, and optimize the content for better engagement and conversion rates. The company tests generative AI to rewrite the existing product descriptions and ads for one of its best-selling smartphones.

Sample Data:

Product: Smartphone - Model X200

Description Type	Before Generative AI	After Generative AI
Title	Smartphone Model X200	Smartphone X200 – Ultimate Power in Your Hands
Short Description	The X200 is a powerful smartphone with great performance and camera quality.	Unleash the power of the X200, featuring groundbreaking speed, a 64MP camera, and a stunning display that will redefine your smartphone experience.
Full Description	The X200 is a smartphone with a fast processor and an excellent camera. It	The X200 is your new ultimate companion with a lightning-fast processor, a 64MP AI-powered camera, and an all-day battery that

Description Type	Before Generative AI	After Generative AI
	has a high-definition screen and long battery life.	keeps you going. With a stunning 6.5-inch AMOLED display and 5G connectivity, it's designed for those who demand the best in performance, style, and functionality.
Ad Copy	Get the powerful X200 smartphone now!	Step into the future with the X200 – Speed, Style, and Power combined. Get yours today and experience tech like never before.
SEO Keywords	smartphone, X200, performance, camera	X200 smartphone, fast processor, 64MP camera, AMOLED display, 5G, best smartphone

Output and Results:

Metric	Before Generative AI	After Generative AI	Change (%)
Engagement Rate	3.2%	5.8%	+81.25%
Click-Through Rate (CTR)	1.5%	2.9%	+93.33%
Conversion Rate	4.0%	6.5%	+62.5%
Average Time on Page	1 min 40 sec	2 min 50 sec	+70.6%
Bounce Rate	45%	33%	-26.7%

Explanation and Interpretation of Results:

- **Engagement Rate**: The increase in engagement indicates that customers are spending more time interacting with the enhanced content, suggesting that the more creative, detailed, and personalized descriptions are resonating better with the audience.

- **Click-Through Rate (CTR)**: The higher CTR suggests that the reworked titles and ad copies are more appealing, likely because they offer more value propositions and include compelling calls to action, which encourage users to click.

- **Conversion Rate**: The increase in conversions implies that users who engage with the enhanced descriptions and ads are more likely to make a purchase, indicating that the generative AI-driven content better addresses customer pain points and aspirations.

- **Average Time on Page**: The longer time on the page suggests that the customers find the enhanced descriptions more informative and engaging, which likely contributes to higher conversion rates.

- **Bounce Rate**: The reduction in bounce rate implies that visitors are more likely to stay on the page after landing, which may be attributed to the more engaging and personalized content created through generative AI.

Observations:

1. **Creativity in Content**: The generative AI transformed basic product descriptions into more engaging, customer-centric narratives that highlighted not only the product's features but also how those features could enhance the customer's lifestyle. This shift seems to resonate more with potential buyers.

2. **SEO Optimization**: By including more specific keywords like "5G," "AMOLED display," and "64MP camera," the product descriptions are better optimized for search engines, improving visibility and driving traffic.

3. **Improved Conversion**: The more detailed and benefit-driven descriptions led to a higher conversion rate. Shoppers were not only more intrigued by the product but also felt more confident in making a purchase due to the clear value proposition communicated through the descriptions.

4. **Customer Retention**: The longer time spent on the page and reduced bounce rate indicate a more engaging user experience, which can help with customer retention and reduce cart abandonment.

Decisions from the E-Commerce Perspective:

1. **Adopt AI-Generated Content Across All Products**: The significant improvements in engagement, conversion, and SEO

suggest that using generative AI for product descriptions and ads is a worthwhile investment. Expanding this practice across more products can further enhance site performance.

2. **Focus on Customer-Centric Messaging**: Moving forward, e-commerce businesses should ensure their product descriptions focus not only on features but on how these features meet customer needs, desires, or solve problems. This customer-first approach seems to resonate strongly with potential buyers.

3. **Continuous Optimization**: AI-driven content creation should be continuously optimized by analyzing performance metrics. Regular A/B testing can be conducted to ensure that the content stays fresh and aligned with customer preferences.

4. **Leverage AI for SEO**: Since generative AI enhances SEO by suggesting relevant keywords and structuring content for better search engine visibility, using AI for ongoing SEO efforts should be a key strategy to increase organic traffic.

Overall, generative AI has the potential to greatly enhance product content for e-commerce sites, making it more compelling, engaging, and optimized for both users and search engines.

1.2 Understanding the Role of AI in E-Commerce

AI has become a driving force in the e-commerce industry, offering retailers innovative ways to improve their operations, customer experience, and overall efficiency. One of the most significant contributions of AI to e-commerce is in the realm of personalization. By analyzing customer behavior, preferences, and past purchasing patterns, AI can provide tailored recommendations and content, helping brands to create more meaningful interactions. This leads to higher engagement rates and boosts sales, as shoppers are presented with products that match their tastes.

Another area where AI is making a difference is in inventory management. Retailers can use AI to predict demand for specific products, optimize stock levels, and reduce overstock or stockout situations. Through the use of machine learning algorithms, e-commerce businesses can analyze data to forecast trends and make more informed decisions about production and procurement. This helps them to streamline operations, reduce waste, and ensure that customers can access the products they want without delay.

AI also plays a crucial role in enhancing the efficiency of customer service. Chatbots and virtual assistants powered by AI can handle a wide range of customer inquiries, from product recommendations to order tracking. These AI systems can operate 24/7, ensuring that customers get quick responses without needing to wait for human agents. This level of responsiveness improves the overall customer experience and frees up human staff to focus on more complex or specialized tasks.

In addition to customer service, AI improves the user experience by optimizing website design and navigation. By studying how users interact with a site, AI can identify patterns and make adjustments to improve the layout or content placement, ensuring that customers can easily find what they are looking for. This not only increases the likelihood of conversions but also enhances user satisfaction, encouraging repeat visits and purchases.

AI-powered advertising is another tool that e-commerce businesses use to increase their reach and effectiveness. Through machine learning, AI can analyze vast amounts of data to identify the most effective advertising strategies for different audiences. It can determine which ads are most likely to resonate with a specific group, adjusting campaigns in real-time to ensure that marketing dollars are spent effectively. This ability to optimize ads in response to changing trends or behaviors results in better-targeted campaigns and higher return on investment.

Finally, fraud detection and security have also benefited from the advancements in AI. With the growing number of online transactions, e-commerce platforms are increasingly vulnerable to fraudulent activities. AI systems can detect unusual patterns in transaction data, flagging potential fraudulent activities before they escalate. These systems can also adapt over time, becoming more effective at identifying new and emerging threats, ensuring that customer data remains secure and the integrity of transactions is maintained.

Practical Example Context: AI-Driven Personalization in E-Commerce

In an e-commerce environment, AI can be used to analyze customer behavior, such as past purchases, product views, and interactions with various categories, to personalize product recommendations. By leveraging machine learning algorithms, the system can predict products a customer is most likely to purchase next, improving both conversion rates and customer satisfaction. The more granular the data, the more accurate the predictions can be, enhancing the shopping experience for the user.

Sample E-Commerce Transaction Data:

Customer ID	Product Viewed	Product Category	Previous Purchase	Total Spend	Session Duration	Recommendation Score
1001	Wireless Earbuds	Electronics	Smartwatch	$200	15 mins	0.85
1002	Running Shoes	Footwear	Running Shorts	$150	10 mins	0.75
1003	Laptop Stand	Electronics	Laptop	$120	12 mins	0.90
1004	Yoga Mat	Sports & Fitness	Dumbbells	$80	18 mins	0.80
1005	Bluetooth Speaker	Electronics	Smart Speaker	$90	20 mins	0.88

AI-Driven Recommendations for Each Customer:

Customer ID	Top 3 Recommended Products	Predicted Category	Reason for Recommendation
1001	Noise Cancelling Headphones, Portable Charger, Fitness Tracker	Electronics, Fitness	High probability of purchasing related electronics due to past purchase of smartwatch and interest in audio products.
1002	Compression Socks, Sports Watch, Yoga Mat	Footwear, Sports & Fitness	Related items based on running shoes view and previous purchase of running shorts, showing interest in active lifestyle products.
1003	Wireless Keyboard, Gaming Mouse, Monitor	Electronics, Gaming	High engagement with laptop-related products indicates a preference for computer accessories, possibly gaming-related based on session duration and spend.
1004	Resistance Bands, Exercise Ball, Sports Water Bottle	Sports & Fitness	Recommendations focus on complementary fitness products, as the user is interested in both yoga mats and dumbbells.
1005	Smart Home Devices, Portable Speakers, Headphones	Electronics, Smart Home	Recommendation based on similar product category (Bluetooth speakers and smart speakers) with an affinity for tech gadgets.

Page| 14

Explanation and Interpretation of Results:

1. **Customer 1001**:
   - The recommendation is based on their interest in electronics, particularly audio products (wireless earbuds and smartwatch). Products such as noise-cancelling headphones and portable chargers are highly relevant.
   - **Action**: Cross-sell accessories like fitness trackers and portable chargers to drive up sales.

2. **Customer 1002**:
   - Since they viewed running shoes and bought running shorts, the AI suggests complementary products like compression socks, sports watches, and yoga mats, which align with an active lifestyle.
   - **Action**: Consider creating personalized bundles or offers combining running shoes, sports accessories, and apparel to increase conversion rates.

3. **Customer 1003**:
   - This user seems interested in laptops and related accessories (laptop stand, wireless keyboard), as well as potential gaming products. The AI recommends items like a gaming mouse or monitor.
   - **Action**: Target them with up-sell opportunities in the gaming and productivity accessory categories.

4. **Customer 1004**:
   - The user has shown interest in both yoga mats and dumbbells, so recommendations focus on fitness-related products such as resistance bands and exercise balls.
   - **Action**: Promote fitness bundles and offer discounts for purchasing complementary items in the fitness category.

5. **Customer 1005**:
   - This user has shown interest in audio tech (Bluetooth speaker, smart speaker) and therefore receives recommendations for similar electronics, like smart home devices and portable speakers.

o **Action**: Upsell or cross-sell more premium audio devices and home automation products, creating an engaging shopping experience.

Observations:

- **Customer behavior patterns** can be observed in the data: previous purchases and product views play a significant role in shaping AI-driven recommendations.

- The **Recommendation Score** is a key metric indicating how likely the customer is to engage with or purchase a suggested product. Higher scores indicate a higher probability of purchase.

- **Personalization** leads to more tailored suggestions, improving customer experience by showing them products they are more likely to buy.

Decisions from the E-Commerce Perspective:

1. **Personalized Offers**: Use AI to craft personalized offers, such as bundling products based on customer behavior.

2. **Cross-Selling**: Introduce complementary products alongside high-interest items (e.g., recommending fitness-related products to users interested in yoga or running).

3. **Upselling**: Recommend premium or upgraded products based on customers' browsing patterns and past purchases.

4. **Improved User Engagement**: Target customers with recommendations aligned with their interests to increase session duration and encourage repeat purchases.

5. **Dynamic Pricing**: Use AI to adjust prices based on customer preferences, behavior, and demand.

By leveraging AI, the e-commerce store can not only enhance the customer experience but also increase conversions, revenue, and customer loyalty through intelligent personalization strategies.

1.3 Key Challenges in Implementing AI in E-Commerce

Implementing AI in e-commerce presents several challenges, starting with the complexity of data integration. E-commerce businesses often rely on multiple platforms, tools, and systems to manage customer interactions, inventory, and transactions. AI solutions must be able to integrate with all these existing systems seamlessly, which can be technically difficult and time-consuming. Companies may face obstacles in consolidating data from various sources, ensuring that it's clean, organized, and ready for AI processing.

Another challenge lies in the quality and quantity of data. AI models rely on large, high-quality datasets to make accurate predictions or recommendations. Many e-commerce businesses struggle with having enough relevant data to train these models effectively. Poor or insufficient data can result in inaccurate insights or recommendations, which can negatively impact customer satisfaction and sales. Additionally, data privacy regulations, such as GDPR, make it crucial for companies to handle customer data responsibly, adding another layer of complexity to AI adoption.

Customer expectations are another hurdle when integrating AI into e-commerce. Shoppers expect personalized experiences, fast responses, and accurate product recommendations. However, AI models must continually learn from consumer behavior and adapt to preferences. If the system's predictions aren't up to par, it can lead to frustration and drive customers away. Furthermore, different customers have unique preferences, so designing AI systems that meet the needs of a broad customer base without overwhelming them with irrelevant suggestions can be challenging.

The cost of implementing AI technology can also be a significant barrier, especially for small to mid-sized e-commerce businesses. While AI can offer tremendous benefits, the upfront investment required for infrastructure, development, and ongoing maintenance is often high. This includes the cost of hiring skilled personnel, purchasing necessary software, and ensuring that AI models are continuously trained and optimized. For many smaller players in the market, these expenses might not seem justifiable, even with the promise of future returns.

Another challenge is the need for specialized skills. Implementing AI in e-commerce requires a team of experts who understand both the technology and the industry. From data scientists to machine learning engineers, the talent pool needed to develop and maintain AI systems can be hard to come by. Smaller e-commerce businesses may struggle to attract and retain this specialized talent, as larger companies tend to offer better compensation and career opportunities. This can make it difficult for businesses to stay competitive in the AI-driven marketplace.

Finally, the evolving nature of AI itself presents a challenge. AI technologies are rapidly changing, and businesses must stay on top of these advancements to avoid becoming outdated. Keeping up with new algorithms, tools, and best practices can be overwhelming, especially for companies that are just beginning to adopt AI. In addition, the fast pace of innovation in AI can lead to shifting expectations, requiring companies to constantly adapt their systems to meet changing demands. This ongoing need for innovation can strain resources and make long-term planning difficult.

Practical Example: Addressing Data Privacy Concerns in AI-Based Personalization for E-Commerce

In e-commerce, AI-driven personalization aims to tailor product recommendations, advertisements, and user experiences based on individual customer data. However, data privacy concerns arise when personal information is collected, stored, and used without explicit consent, potentially violating customer trust and regulatory guidelines (e.g., GDPR). The goal is to balance delivering personalized experiences while protecting customer privacy. For example, consider a clothing retailer that collects data such as purchase history, browsing behavior, and demographic information for personalizing recommendations. The company implements a privacy-preserving approach by anonymizing sensitive data and allowing users to opt in or out of data sharing for personalized experiences.

Sample Data

Customer ID	Name	Age	Gender	Browsing History	Purchase History	Opt-in for Personalization	Data Anonymized
101	Alice	28	Female	"Dresses, Summer Collection"	"Red Dress, Floral Skirt"	Yes	Yes
102	Bob	34	Male	"Sports Shoes,	"Running Shoes,	No	Yes

Custom er ID	Name	Age	Gender	Browsing History	Purchase History	Opt-in for Personalization	Data Anonymized
				Running Gear"	Sweatshirt"		
103	Charlie	22	Male	"Laptops, Tech Gadgets"	"Laptop, Wireless Mouse"	Yes	Yes
104	Diana	40	Female	"Handbags, Leather Accessories"	"Leather Bag, Wallet"	Yes	Yes
105	Eva	30	Female	"Winter Jackets, Boots"	"Winter Jacket, Boots"	No	Yes

Output and Results

Customer ID	Personalized Recommendations	Privacy Preserving Mechanism	Conversion Rate	Customer Feedback
101	"Floral Skirt", "Summer Dress"	Anonymized Data, Opt-in for Personalization	25%	Positive
102	None	Opt-out of Personalization	0%	Neutral
103	"Wireless Earbuds", "Laptop Bag"	Anonymized Data, Opt-in for Personalization	30%	Positive
104	"Leather Purse", "Winter Gloves"	Anonymized Data, Opt-in for Personalization	22%	Positive

Customer ID	Personalized Recommendations	Privacy Preserving Mechanism	Conversion Rate	Customer Feedback
105	None	Opt-out of Personalization	0%	Negative

Explanation and Interpretation of Results

- **Customer Preferences and Conversion Rate**: Customers who opted into data-sharing for personalized recommendations (e.g., Alice, Charlie, Diana) showed a higher conversion rate (ranging from 22% to 30%) compared to customers who opted out (e.g., Bob, Eva), who had a 0% conversion rate. This highlights that personalization drives engagement and sales, but only when customers consent to sharing their data.

- **Privacy Mechanism Impact**: The company's anonymization of sensitive data ensures that even customers who opt into personalization have their data protected. The fact that conversion rates are still decent for opt-in customers indicates that the privacy-preserving mechanisms are effective in building trust.

- **Customer Feedback**: Positive feedback from customers who opted in shows a higher satisfaction with personalized experiences. Conversely, those who opted out (e.g., Bob, Eva) exhibited neutral or negative feedback, indicating that the lack of personalized recommendations leads to dissatisfaction or frustration with the shopping experience.

Observations

1. **Customer Trust is Crucial**: Customers who feel their data is safe and have control over how it is used are more likely to engage with personalized content.

2. **Opt-in vs. Opt-out**: The higher conversion rates among customers who opt-in suggests that customers are willing to share their data when they see value, but privacy remains a critical factor in their decision.

3. **Impact of Anonymization**: The anonymization of data ensures that even with personalization, customers' sensitive information is not exposed, which helps mitigate privacy concerns.

Decisions from the E-Commerce Perspective

1. **Clear Communication**: Ensure that customers are fully aware of what data is being collected and how it will be used. This transparency can increase trust and encourage opt-ins.

2. **Incentivize Opt-ins**: Offer benefits or discounts for customers who consent to data-sharing, while also making it clear that data will be anonymized and used responsibly.

3. **Customization without Intrusion**: Personalization should never feel invasive. Offering limited personalization for users who opt out could help increase overall satisfaction, even if conversion rates are lower.

4. **Privacy Protection**: Continuously monitor and update privacy practices to comply with regulations and to maintain customer trust, ensuring that anonymized data is secure and handled responsibly.

By balancing personalization with privacy, e-commerce companies can build a loyal customer base while driving sales growth.

2. Collection and Management in E-Commerce

Collection and management in e-commerce play crucial roles in ensuring smooth operations and customer satisfaction. The first step in managing e-commerce transactions involves efficient collection of orders, which includes both processing customer requests and ensuring payment.

When a customer places an order online, the system must accurately capture the details, including product specifications, payment methods, and shipping information. This data is then used to confirm the transaction and prepare for the next steps in order fulfillment. A reliable collection system helps to minimize errors and delays in processing orders, which can significantly impact customer experience.

Once an order is placed, the management process takes over, which includes inventory tracking, order processing, and fulfillment. Managing inventory is one of the most vital aspects of e-commerce operations, as it ensures that the products advertised on the website are available for customers. With real-time tracking systems, e-commerce businesses can monitor stock levels and automatically update product availability. This allows companies to avoid overselling or understocking items, ensuring that orders can be processed promptly without unexpected delays.

The next critical aspect of collection and management is payment processing. E-commerce businesses rely on various payment gateways to securely handle transactions. This process involves the verification of payment details, processing the transaction, and confirming that the customer's payment has been successfully received. Managing different payment methods, such as credit cards, digital wallets, and bank transfers, adds complexity but is essential to cater to a wide customer base. Handling refunds, chargebacks, and disputes also becomes part of the overall management, requiring efficient customer support and financial systems to maintain trust.

Shipping and logistics are integral parts of managing e-commerce operations. Once payment is confirmed, the next step is shipping the product to the customer. This process involves selecting the right courier, managing shipping costs, and ensuring timely delivery. Proper management ensures that the product reaches the customer without damage, within the expected time frame, and at the correct address. E-commerce businesses often collaborate with third-party logistics companies to streamline these processes, offering tracking services and real-time updates to customers, enhancing their experience and reducing the likelihood of complaints.

Customer service and after-sales support are also essential components of e-commerce management. Customers often require assistance with order issues, returns, exchanges, or questions about products. An effective customer service team can resolve issues quickly, increasing customer loyalty and preventing negative reviews. Proper management of returns and exchanges ensures that customers are satisfied with their purchase experience. A well-organized return policy and seamless process can improve customer retention, as shoppers feel more confident about making a purchase when they know they can easily return or exchange products if needed.

Lastly, data collection and analysis are indispensable in managing e-commerce operations. By tracking customer behavior, sales trends, and operational performance, businesses can identify areas for improvement and opportunities for growth. Data analysis helps in making informed decisions regarding product assortment, pricing strategies, marketing campaigns, and customer engagement. Over time, effective use of data can lead to better targeting of customer segments, personalized shopping experiences, and improved overall business performance. Managing data responsibly also ensures compliance with privacy regulations and builds customer trust.

Practical Example of Collection and Management in E-Commerce

In an e-commerce business, managing customer data, purchase behavior, and inventory is essential for making informed decisions. For instance, an online store selling electronic gadgets needs to collect and manage data about customer purchases, preferences, and product inventory levels to optimize sales, stock management, and marketing efforts. Consider a company that collects data on monthly sales of three different products over the last quarter. This data is essential to identify trends, demand forecasting, and adjusting inventory accordingly.

Sample Data:

Product Name	Units Sold (Jan)	Units Sold (Feb)	Units Sold (Mar)	Total Units Sold	Average Monthly Sales	Stock Available	Stock Shortage (if any)
Smartwatch	150	120	180	450	150	200	0
Bluetooth Earbuds	200	220	180	600	200	100	100
Laptop	80	60	100	240	80	50	50

Output and Results

1. **Smartwatch:**
   - o   Total units sold: 450 units over 3 months
   - o   Average monthly sales: 150 units
   - o   Stock available: 200 units
   - o   No stock shortage.

2. **Bluetooth Earbuds:**
   - o   Total units sold: 600 units over 3 months
   - o   Average monthly sales: 200 units
   - o   Stock available: 100 units

> o Stock shortage: 100 units (need 200 units to meet demand).

3. **Laptop:**
   - o Total units sold: 240 units over 3 months
   - o Average monthly sales: 80 units
   - o Stock available: 50 units
   - o Stock shortage: 50 units (need 100 units to meet demand).

Explanation and Interpretation:

- **Smartwatch**: Sales are stable and the stock is sufficient to meet demand. There's no immediate need to adjust inventory levels for this product.

- **Bluetooth Earbuds**: The product is in high demand, and the current stock is insufficient to cover the next month's sales. There's a shortage of 100 units, suggesting the need to reorder and possibly scale up production.

- **Laptop**: The stock is also running low (50 units available vs. 100 units needed), indicating the need to replenish inventory to avoid stockouts.

Observations:

1. **Demand vs. Stock**: Products like Bluetooth Earbuds and Laptops are facing potential stockouts, while the Smartwatch has sufficient stock.

2. **Sales Trends**: The Bluetooth Earbuds have shown consistent demand, with the highest sales in February. This suggests that the marketing or promotional efforts for this product may be successful and should be continued.

3. **Stock Management**: For products with shortages (Earbuds and Laptops), inventory levels should be monitored closely to avoid disappointing customers and lost sales.

Decisions from an E-Commerce Perspective:

1. **Replenish Inventory**: For products with shortages (Bluetooth Earbuds and Laptops), it's crucial to reorder supplies to prevent stockouts.

2. **Analyze Sales and Marketing**: Since the Bluetooth Earbuds are consistently popular, there might be a need to consider increasing the order quantity or even marketing the product more heavily.

3. **Stock Optimization**: For products like the Smartwatch, the company might consider slowing down restocking efforts unless a spike in demand is predicted, as the current stock is sufficient.

4. **Promotions and Forecasting**: Predict future trends and ensure adequate stock levels for high-demand products during seasonal sales or promotional periods.

This data collection and management approach helps businesses stay agile and make data-driven decisions for better operational efficiency.

2.1 Types of Data Collected in E-Commerce

In e-commerce, a wide variety of data is collected to better understand customers, improve user experience, and optimize business operations. One key type of data is personal information, such as names, addresses, email addresses, and phone numbers. This data helps businesses create customer profiles, communicate with users, and ensure that products are delivered to the right locations. It also aids in personalized marketing, where businesses tailor their messages and promotions to individual preferences and demographics.

Another important type of data is transaction data. This includes purchase details such as the products customers buy, their quantities, prices, and the method of payment. Transaction data is crucial for analyzing sales trends, managing inventory, and understanding customer buying behavior. It also plays a role in generating receipts, processing refunds, and managing financial records for both the customer and the business.

Behavioral data is collected through tracking technologies like cookies, analytics tools, and user activity logs. This data includes information on how customers interact with a website, such as the pages they visit, the products they view, the time they spend on certain pages, and their navigation patterns. By understanding these behaviors, businesses can enhance website usability, personalize user experiences, and identify potential pain points in the customer journey that could lead to cart abandonment or frustration.

Customer feedback is another valuable type of data. This includes reviews, ratings, surveys, and direct feedback provided through customer service channels. This data helps e-commerce businesses gauge customer satisfaction, identify areas for improvement, and refine their products or services. Positive feedback can also be leveraged for marketing purposes, building social proof and trust with prospective buyers.

Shipping and logistics data is essential for tracking order fulfillment and delivery processes. Information such as shipping addresses, delivery preferences, tracking numbers, and shipping carrier details is gathered to ensure orders are processed and delivered on time. This data also allows businesses to handle customer inquiries related to order status and resolve any issues regarding lost or delayed shipments.

Lastly, inventory data plays a critical role in e-commerce operations. Businesses track product availability, stock levels, and supply chain information to avoid running out of popular products or overstocking items that are not in demand. Real-time inventory data helps businesses manage restocking, forecast demand, and make informed purchasing decisions, ultimately improving profitability and customer satisfaction.

Practical Example:

In the context of an e-commerce platform, understanding customer behavior and product information is key to providing personalized recommendations and improving customer satisfaction. Structured data refers to well-organized and easily interpretable data, such as transactional records (e.g., customer purchases, product details). On the other hand, unstructured data includes free-text feedback like customer reviews. Integrating both types of data allows for deeper insights into customer preferences and product performance, leading to better decision-making.

Sample Dataset:

Structured Data (Transactional Data):

Order ID	Customer ID	Product ID	Product Name	Price	Quantity	Total Value	Order Date
1001	C001	P101	Wireless Mouse	25.00	1	25.00	2025-01-01
1002	C002	P102	Bluetooth Keyboard	45.00	2	90.00	2025-01-02
1003	C003	P103	Laptop Stand	30.00	1	30.00	2025-01-03
1004	C004	P104	Office Chair	150.00	1	150.00	2025-01-04
1005	C005	P105	Monitor	200.00	1	200.00	2025-01-05

Unstructured Data (Customer Reviews):

Review ID	Customer ID	Product ID	Review Text	Rating
R001	C001	P101	"Great mouse, smooth control and ergonomic design."	4

Review ID	Customer ID	Product ID	Review Text	Rating
R002	C002	P102	"Good keyboard but a bit loud while typing."	3
R003	C003	P103	"The stand is sturdy and helps with posture improvement."	5
R004	C004	P104	"Comfortable chair, but not great for long hours of sitting."	3
R005	C005	P105	"Amazing monitor with great picture quality for work and gaming."	5

Integrating Structured and Unstructured Data:

By analyzing both datasets, e-commerce platforms can draw insights on which products are most popular, which ones receive positive or negative feedback, and how customer behavior correlates with reviews.

1. **Product Performance**:
   - Product P101 (Wireless Mouse) has a good rating (4) with a positive review about its smooth control and ergonomic design. This suggests that the product is performing well and might appeal to a broader audience.
   - Product P102 (Bluetooth Keyboard) has a rating of 3, indicating mixed feedback due to noise while typing. This could be addressed through a product improvement or highlighting the feature in marketing.

2. **Customer Behavior**:
   - Customer C001 purchased the wireless mouse and left a positive review. Analyzing such patterns can help identify loyal customers who are satisfied with products.
   - Customers who purchased higher-value products (e.g., P104, P105) like the office chair and monitor have also left positive feedback, possibly because these are more significant investments, and the reviews reflect greater satisfaction.

Output and Results (Summary):

Product Name	Avg. Rating	Total Sales Value	Quantity Sold	Avg. Price	Positive Feedback (%)	Negative Feedback (%)
Wireless Mouse	4.0	25.00	1	25.00	100%	0%
Bluetooth Keyboard	3.0	90.00	2	45.00	50%	50%
Laptop Stand	5.0	30.00	1	30.00	100%	0%
Office Chair	3.0	150.00	1	150.00	50%	50%
Monitor	5.0	200.00	1	200.00	100%	0%

Observations:

- Products with higher ratings (e.g., Laptop Stand, Monitor) align with higher customer satisfaction, indicating positive customer experience.

- Products like the Bluetooth Keyboard and Office Chair have a lower rating, suggesting areas for improvement or different marketing strategies.

- The average price correlates with higher sales value, but the feedback quality impacts customer loyalty and satisfaction.

Decisions from an E-Commerce Perspective:

1. **Product Improvement**: Based on customer reviews, the Bluetooth Keyboard and Office Chair need improvements. The keyboard's loud typing sound and the chair's comfort level for long hours should be addressed to enhance the product offering.

2. **Marketing Focus**: Products with high ratings (Wireless Mouse, Monitor) should be emphasized in marketing campaigns to boost their sales further. Highlighting customer satisfaction will likely attract more buyers.

3. **Customer Loyalty Programs**: Identifying satisfied customers (C001, C003, C005) can help personalize marketing efforts and develop loyalty programs, especially for high-value purchases.

4. **Product Diversification**: The integration of reviews with transactional data can also suggest opportunities to diversify the product range to meet emerging customer needs.

By leveraging both structured and unstructured data, e-commerce platforms can make data-driven decisions that improve customer experience and drive sales growth.

2.2 Data Management Strategies for E-Commerce

Data management is crucial for e-commerce businesses as they generate large volumes of data from transactions, customer behavior, and inventory. The ability to collect, organize, and analyze this data allows businesses to improve customer experiences, streamline operations, and increase profitability. A key strategy involves using data management platforms that can consolidate data from multiple sources into a centralized system. This ensures that data is accessible, consistent, and accurate, which is vital for making informed decisions and enhancing business strategies.

To effectively manage data, e-commerce businesses need to adopt proper data governance practices. This includes establishing clear policies and guidelines for data collection, storage, and usage. It helps prevent data breaches, ensures compliance with privacy laws, and improves the overall quality of data. By keeping data organized and secure, businesses reduce the risk of errors and inefficiencies that could harm customer trust or lead to lost opportunities.

Another important aspect of data management is data integration. E-commerce platforms often deal with a variety of systems, such as customer relationship management (CRM), inventory management, and marketing tools. Integrating these systems ensures that data flows seamlessly across different departments, which helps in creating a more cohesive strategy for customer engagement and inventory management. Effective integration can also lead to more accurate forecasting and real-time insights, which are essential in a fast-moving e-commerce environment.

Data analytics plays a significant role in e-commerce data management by allowing businesses to extract valuable insights from the data. By using advanced analytics tools, businesses can better understand customer behavior, track purchasing patterns, and identify market trends. These insights help in personalizing the shopping experience, optimizing pricing strategies, and improving product recommendations. Ultimately, leveraging data analytics can lead to better decision-making, increased customer satisfaction, and higher conversion rates.

Data privacy and security are significant concerns for e-commerce businesses as they handle sensitive customer information. Implementing robust security measures, such as encryption and secure access controls, helps protect data from unauthorized access and cyber threats. Additionally, businesses need to comply with data protection regulations, such as GDPR, to ensure that customer data is handled with the utmost care and transparency. Ensuring data privacy and security strengthens customer trust and loyalty, which is crucial for long-term success.

Finally, businesses must ensure that their data management strategies remain scalable as they grow. As the e-commerce business expands, the volume and complexity of data will increase. By adopting scalable solutions, businesses can ensure that they can manage and leverage their data without encountering performance issues. This includes choosing cloud-based data storage systems and automated tools that can handle the growing demands of the business while maintaining data integrity and accessibility.

Practical Example: Building a Centralized Data Warehouse for E-Commerce Transaction and Behavior Data

In this scenario, an e-commerce company seeks to create a centralized data warehouse to aggregate customer transaction and behavior data from multiple sources, such as website interactions, purchase data, and customer service logs. The goal is to analyze customer behavior, track purchases, and optimize marketing strategies. By integrating data from various sources, such as website analytics, transaction logs, and customer surveys, the company aims to gain actionable insights that will drive sales, improve customer satisfaction, and personalize marketing efforts.

Sample Data Architecture

The data is collected from three main sources:

1. **Website Analytics**: Tracks user interactions, such as page views, session duration, and clicks.

2. **Customer Transactions**: Stores details of the customer's purchases, such as product name, quantity, and total value.

3. **Customer Service Logs**: Records customer support inquiries, including ticket IDs, query types, and response times.

Sample Data

Customer ID	Date	Product Name	Category	Purchase Amount	Website Session Duration (minutes)	Support Tickets Opened	Last Login Date
101	2025-01-10	Wireless Mouse	Electronics	29.99	15	1	2025-01-09
102	2025-01-10	Laptop Stand	Accessories	49.99	30	0	2025-01-10
103	2025-01-11	Smart Watch	Wearables	199.99	45	2	2025-01-11
104	2025-01-12	Gaming Chair	Furniture	179.99	20	1	2025-01-12
105	2025-01-13	Bluetooth Speaker	Electronics	79.99	35	0	2025-01-13

Output and Results

After integrating the data, the data warehouse can be queried to derive key insights:

1. **Total Sales per Category**:
   o Electronics: $109.98
   o Accessories: $49.99
   o Wearables: $199.99
   o Furniture: $179.99
2. **Average Session Duration** by Category:
   o Electronics: 25 minutes

- Accessories: 30 minutes
- Wearables: 45 minutes
- Furniture: 20 minutes

3. **Customer Service Tickets Analysis**:
   - Customers with multiple support tickets: 2 (Customer IDs 103 and 104)
   - Customers with no support tickets: 3 (Customer IDs 101, 102, and 105)

Interpretation of Results

1. **Sales Insights**:
   - **Highest sales** come from Wearables and Furniture, indicating these categories are popular among customers.
   - Electronics also perform well but with a lower total amount compared to the other two.

2. **Session Duration Insights**:
   - Customers browsing Wearables spend more time on the site, which might suggest that they are engaging more deeply with product information or features.
   - The **shorter session durations** in the Furniture category suggest that customers may be less interested or browsing less intensely in this category.

3. **Customer Service Insights**:
   - Customers with multiple support tickets (e.g., Customer 103 and Customer 104) may indicate issues with product quality or customer experience, requiring further investigation.

Observations and Decisions from an E-Commerce Perspective

- **Product Category Focus**: Based on sales, the company should consider promoting Wearables and Furniture more actively, as these categories are driving significant revenue.
- **Session Engagement**: The longer session duration in Wearables suggests the need for deeper engagement tactics such as personalized recommendations or tutorials for customers in that category.

- **Customer Service Focus**: Customers with multiple support tickets should be prioritized for follow-up, possibly through targeted surveys or improved customer service processes to enhance their experience.

- **Marketing Strategy**: Personalized marketing campaigns for customers who spend longer sessions on specific categories could help drive conversions. Retargeting ads or email campaigns can be designed based on the products viewed or purchased.

Final Decision:

The company should leverage data from the centralized data warehouse to tailor marketing, improve product offerings, and enhance customer service. By focusing on the high-performing categories (Wearables and Furniture) and addressing potential customer service bottlenecks, the e-commerce platform can boost sales and customer satisfaction.

2.3 Data Privacy and Security Concerns in E-Commerce

In the rapidly evolving world of e-commerce, data privacy and security have become significant concerns for both consumers and businesses. With the increase in online transactions, personal and financial data are frequently exchanged, making it crucial for companies to ensure the protection of sensitive information. Customers expect their details, including credit card numbers, addresses, and browsing history, to be kept private and secure from unauthorized access. As cyber threats evolve, businesses face mounting pressure to adopt robust measures to safeguard their systems against breaches.

Hackers continuously exploit vulnerabilities in e-commerce platforms, using advanced methods to access and steal consumer data. This has led to a rise in data breaches, where personal information, such as names, passwords, and payment details, is exposed. When a breach occurs, it can significantly damage the reputation of an e-commerce company, erode customer trust, and result in costly legal consequences. In some cases, consumers may fall victim to identity theft or fraud, further increasing the stakes for businesses to invest in secure technologies.

The rise of online shopping has also prompted discussions on data collection practices. E-commerce businesses often gather vast amounts of data on their users to personalize shopping experiences, improve recommendations, and optimize marketing efforts. While this data can enhance the customer experience, it raises concerns about how much information is being collected and whether consumers are aware of the extent of this collection. Many consumers are uncomfortable with the level of surveillance that some companies maintain, fearing that their data could be misused, sold, or shared without their consent.

Privacy regulations such as the General Data Protection Regulation (GDPR) in the European Union and the California Consumer Privacy Act (CCPA) in the United States have been enacted to address these concerns. These laws impose strict requirements on businesses to protect consumer data, obtain clear consent for data collection, and allow customers to access or delete their information upon request. E-commerce businesses must comply with these regulations, but the complexity and varying standards across jurisdictions can pose challenges. Non-compliance can result in heavy fines, making adherence a critical consideration for any company operating in the global market.

To combat data security risks, e-commerce platforms must invest in encryption technologies, secure payment gateways, and regular security audits. Encryption ensures that any sensitive data transferred between the customer and the website is unreadable to potential attackers. Payment gateways play a key role in securing transactions, providing an added layer of protection by processing payments separately from the main e-commerce platform. Additionally, businesses need to implement multi-factor authentication, strong password policies, and employee training to reduce the risk of internal security threats.

Finally, consumer awareness is a vital element in maintaining data privacy and security. While businesses play a large role in protecting customer information, consumers must also take precautions to safeguard their personal data. Simple measures such as using strong passwords, being cautious of phishing attacks, and regularly monitoring financial statements can help mitigate risks. E-commerce businesses should educate their customers about the importance of data security and offer transparent policies regarding data usage and protection. Building trust through transparency and security practices is essential for long-term success in the e-commerce industry.

Practical Example

In the context of e-commerce, ensuring secure transactions and data encryption is crucial to protecting customer data and preventing fraud. AI-driven security tools are used to analyze transaction patterns in real-time, identifying unusual behavior or potential fraud. For instance, an AI system can analyze factors such as the frequency of purchases, the customer's location, and past purchasing patterns to detect anomalies and flag suspicious transactions. A practical example involves an AI tool monitoring transaction data for a sample e-commerce site.

Sample Data (Transaction Data):

Transaction ID	Customer ID	Transaction Amount	Location	Payment Method	Frequency of Purchases (per month)	Time of Transaction	AI Flagged as Fraud
T001	C123	$120	New York	Credit Card	5	10:05 AM	No

Transaction ID	Customer ID	Transaction Amount	Location	Payment Method	Frequency of Purchases (per month)	Time of Transaction	AI Flagged as Fraud
T002	C123	$3000	New York	Credit Card	5	10:10 AM	Yes
T003	C124	$50	California	PayPal	2	1:30 PM	No
T004	C125	$450	London	Debit Card	3	2:45 PM	No
T005	C126	$9000	New York	Credit Card	12	9:00 AM	Yes

Output and Results (Fraud Detection):

Transaction ID	AI Flagged as Fraud	Reason for Flagging	Confidence Level	Action Taken
T001	No	Normal behavior	98%	Processed
T002	Yes	Unusual high transaction	99%	Held for review
T003	No	Normal behavior	95%	Processed
T004	No	Normal behavior	96%	Processed
T005	Yes	Unusual high transaction	98%	Held for review

Explanation and Interpretation of Results:

1. **Transaction T001 (Normal)**: The AI system did not flag this transaction as fraud. The amount is typical for the customer's

transaction history, and the confidence level in this decision was 98%, indicating a low risk.

2. **Transaction T002 (Fraud Detected)**: This transaction of $3000 was flagged as fraud by the AI system due to the unusually high amount compared to the customer's typical spending. The system's confidence in this detection was 99%, which is high. Therefore, the transaction was held for review.

3. **Transaction T003 (Normal)**: This $50 purchase from California was flagged as legitimate. Despite being from a different location, the transaction amount and purchasing frequency aligned with past patterns, so the confidence level was 95%.

4. **Transaction T004 (Normal)**: A $450 purchase from London was processed without any flags. The confidence in this decision was 96%, indicating that this transaction did not deviate from the customer's behavior.

5. **Transaction T005 (Fraud Detected)**: This high-value transaction of $9000 was flagged due to the sharp increase in spending, as well as the customer's purchase history. With a confidence level of 98%, the AI system determined this to be suspicious and suggested holding it for review.

Observations:

- **High-Value Transactions**: Transactions with unusually high amounts relative to previous spending patterns were flagged for review (T002, T005).

- **Confidence Level**: High confidence levels (above 95%) were associated with accurate fraud detection.

- **Location and Frequency**: The AI system did not flag transactions purely based on location (e.g., T003), but focused on patterns of spending behavior and frequency.

Decisions from the E-Commerce Perspective:

- **Hold Suspicious Transactions**: Transactions flagged as potentially fraudulent (e.g., T002, T005) should be temporarily held until further review, ensuring that the customer's identity and transaction legitimacy are verified before processing.

- **Leverage AI for Real-Time Fraud Prevention**: Use AI tools to continuously monitor transactions and flag suspicious activity in real-time. This minimizes risks associated with delayed fraud detection.

- **Continuous Training of AI Models**: As fraud techniques evolve, the AI model should be continuously trained with new transaction data and fraud patterns to improve its accuracy.

- **Enhance Customer Verification**: For flagged transactions, an additional layer of customer verification (e.g., 2FA or identity checks) should be introduced to confirm legitimacy before completing the purchase.

By adopting AI-driven security tools, e-commerce platforms can significantly reduce fraudulent activities and ensure secure transactions, providing a safer experience for both businesses and customers.

3. Personalized Marketing with AI

Personalized marketing using AI is a strategy that leverages data analysis and machine learning to tailor content, recommendations, and advertisements to individual customers. This process begins by collecting data about customer behaviors, preferences, and past interactions. AI tools analyze this data to identify patterns and trends that can inform how brands should communicate with their audience, ultimately making the experience more relevant and engaging.

One of the key advantages of AI in personalized marketing is its ability to automate and scale the creation of personalized content. Instead of manually crafting unique campaigns for each customer, AI algorithms can generate personalized messages or product recommendations at scale, adjusting content dynamically based on the customer's preferences. This reduces the time and effort needed for customization while increasing the effectiveness of marketing efforts.

AI can also enhance customer segmentation. Traditional segmentation relies on broad demographic data, but with AI, businesses can segment their audience based on more intricate behavior and interests. This leads to more precise targeting, ensuring that each segment receives content that speaks directly to their needs or desires. For example, AI can analyze a customer's previous purchases and browsing history to predict what products they are most likely to buy next.

In addition, AI-driven personalization improves customer experiences across multiple touchpoints, such as websites, email marketing, and social media. AI can adapt in real-time to how a customer interacts with a brand, offering personalized product suggestions or content as they browse. This creates a smoother and more consistent experience, which increases the likelihood of customer satisfaction and loyalty.

Another powerful aspect of AI in personalized marketing is predictive analytics. By examining historical data, AI can forecast future customer behaviors, such as when a customer is likely to make a purchase or which products they might be interested in. This insight allows businesses to proactively target customers with relevant offers or content, leading to higher conversion rates and more efficient marketing campaigns.

Finally, personalized marketing with AI can lead to better customer retention. By continually offering tailored experiences, brands can make customers feel valued and understood, which fosters long-term loyalty. AI also enables brands to track and measure customer responses to personalized campaigns, providing valuable feedback that can be used to refine and improve future marketing efforts. In this way, AI helps businesses maintain a cycle of continuous improvement, ensuring that their marketing remains effective and relevant.

Practical Example of Personalized Marketing with AI

In an e-commerce store selling clothing, AI-driven personalized marketing is implemented to recommend products to customers based on their browsing history, purchase behavior, and demographic data. The AI algorithm analyzes customer data to create personalized product suggestions, tailored to the preferences and interests of each customer. In this case, we have a sample group of customers, and the AI generates recommendations based on past purchase behavior. The goal is to increase sales conversion rates and customer satisfaction.

Sample Data:

Customer ID	Age	Gender	Browsing History	Previous Purchases	AI Recommendation	Conversion Rate (%)
001	25	Male	T-shirts, Hoodies, Sneakers	T-shirt, Sneakers	Hoodie, Sneakers, Joggers	40
002	34	Female	Dresses, Skirts, Blouses	Dress, Blouse	Skirt, Blouse, Shoes	55
003	45	Female	Coats, Jackets, Boots	Coat, Boots	Jackets, Scarf, Turtleneck Sweater	50
004	29	Male	Jeans, Casual Shirts, Jackets	Jeans, Shirt	Jacket, Casual Shoes, Polo Shirt	30
005	40	Male	Sweaters, Jackets, Shoes	Sweater, Shoes	Jacket, Boots, T-shirt	60

AI Output & Results:

The AI has recommended products based on the customer's past behavior and preferences:

- **Customer 001**: Predicted to buy hoodies and joggers based on previous purchases of sneakers and t-shirts. The conversion rate is 40%, meaning 40% of customers who received similar recommendations made a purchase.

- **Customer 002**: Recommended skirts and shoes after purchasing dresses and blouses. This customer's higher conversion rate (55%) indicates a more likely purchase based on the tailored suggestions.

- **Customer 003**: Suggestions like jackets and scarves reflect the customer's interest in coats and boots. The conversion rate of 50% suggests moderate success in influencing purchases.

- **Customer 004**: Personalized recommendations for jackets and casual shoes had a conversion rate of 30%, indicating lower success in matching preferences.

- **Customer 005**: With a higher conversion rate of 60%, personalized product suggestions for boots and jackets are aligned with previous purchases and interests, making the recommendations highly relevant.

Observations & Analysis:

1. **Customer Preferences Matter**: Customers with a high conversion rate (e.g., Customer 005) tend to have a consistent past behavior, where AI's product recommendations are closely aligned with previous purchases.

2. **Age and Gender Influence**: The AI's suggestions are better when it considers demographic data like age and gender. Female customers (e.g., Customer 002 and 003) showed a more consistent response to the recommendations, possibly due to more defined preferences in clothing.

3. **Product Relevance**: Customers with more varied browsing and purchase history (e.g., Customer 001) had lower conversion rates, possibly because the AI's suggestions were too diverse or less focused.

E-Commerce Perspective Decisions:

1. **Segmented Marketing**: For higher conversion rates, segment customers based on demographic and behavioral data. Offer more personalized product recommendations to age and gender groups that show more predictable patterns.

2. **Behavioral Analysis**: Improve AI algorithms by factoring in more granular browsing patterns (e.g., specific clothing items), ensuring the recommendations are more tailored and relevant.

3. **Refinement of Product Suggestions**: If a customer has a low conversion rate, adjust the AI recommendations to focus more on their previously purchased items or more popular products within their browsing categories.

4. **Testing & Optimization**: Continuously test and adjust the AI model's accuracy in predicting purchases. Regular feedback and A/B testing can enhance the relevance of suggestions, improving overall customer engagement and sales.

In conclusion, personalized marketing through AI can significantly boost conversion rates when tailored recommendations are based on both demographic and behavioral data. However, continuous optimization and segmentation are crucial for maintaining and improving these results.

3.1 AI-Driven Customer Segmentation

AI-driven customer segmentation uses advanced machine learning algorithms to analyze and categorize customers based on various attributes such as behavior, demographics, purchasing patterns, and preferences. This technology goes beyond traditional segmentation methods by identifying subtle, hidden patterns within vast amounts of data that would be impossible to detect manually. With AI, companies can segment their customer base more accurately and efficiently, ensuring they can target the right audience with personalized experiences.

The process starts with gathering data from multiple sources, including transactions, website visits, social media activity, and customer feedback. AI algorithms then process this data, identifying significant trends and correlations that help group customers into distinct segments. These segments can be based on factors like age, income, buying frequency, or even the likelihood of a customer churning. The more granular and diverse the data, the better AI can classify the customer base.

One of the major advantages of AI-driven segmentation is its ability to continuously update and refine customer segments. As new data comes in, machine learning models can adjust the segments in real-time, adapting to changing customer behaviors or market conditions. This dynamic segmentation helps businesses stay relevant and proactive, making it possible to launch targeted campaigns or product offerings that align with current customer needs and preferences.

AI also brings the ability to predict future customer behavior. By analyzing historical data, machine learning algorithms can forecast which customers are most likely to make a purchase, engage with a marketing campaign, or even stop using a product or service. These predictions allow companies to make data-driven decisions, focusing their resources on the customers who are most valuable and minimizing wasted efforts on less engaged segments.

Another significant benefit is the improved personalization that AI provides. By creating highly specific segments, companies can tailor their marketing, sales, and customer service strategies to each group's unique characteristics. Whether it's recommending products, adjusting communication styles, or offering customized promotions, AI helps businesses deliver highly relevant and engaging experiences for their customers, increasing loyalty and satisfaction.

Lastly, AI-driven segmentation can also drive operational efficiency. Instead of relying on manual processes or broad demographic categories, businesses can automate much of the segmentation work, freeing up resources to focus on more strategic tasks. Additionally, with more accurate targeting, companies can improve their return on investment (ROI) for marketing and sales efforts, ensuring that every interaction with a customer is purposeful and impactful.

Practical Example of K-Means Clustering for Customer Segmentation in E-Commerce

In an e-commerce setting, businesses often use K-Means clustering to segment their customers into distinct groups based on demographic data and purchase history to run targeted marketing campaigns. This allows for more personalized strategies and increased marketing ROI. For example, suppose an e-commerce company wants to categorize its customers into different clusters based on age, annual income, and total spending over the last year. By using K-Means clustering, the company can identify segments that may have distinct preferences and behaviors, enabling them to tailor their campaigns accordingly.

Sample Customer Data

Customer ID	Age	Annual Income (USD)	Total Spending (USD)
1	25	40,000	500
2	35	60,000	1,500
3	45	80,000	3,000
4	55	100,000	5,000
5	30	50,000	800
6	40	70,000	2,000
7	50	90,000	4,000
8	60	120,000	6,000
9	29	55,000	1,000
10	36	65,000	1,700

Applying K-Means Clustering (with 3 clusters)

After applying K-Means clustering (with k=3 clusters), the data might result in the following cluster assignments and centroids:

Cluster	Customer IDs	Average Age	Average Income (USD)	Average Spending (USD)
1	1, 5, 9	28	48,333	766.67
2	2, 6, 10	34	63,667	1,500
3	3, 4, 7, 8	48.5	95,000	4,750

Interpretation and Observations:

1. **Cluster 1** (Young, Low Spend):
   - These customers are relatively young (around 28 years old) with lower annual incomes (around $48,333) and lower total spending on the platform (~$766).
   - **Marketing Decision**: The company can offer discounts, budget-friendly product recommendations, or loyalty programs to encourage higher spending and repeat purchases.

2. **Cluster 2** (Middle-Aged, Medium Spend):
   - Customers in this cluster are in their mid-30s with a moderate annual income (Income 63,667 and spending 1,500).
   - **Marketing Decision**: Target these customers with mid-range products or seasonal offers that align with their buying power, potentially introducing product bundles or promotions that increase spending.

3. **Cluster 3** (Older, High Spend):
   - These customers are older (around 48 years old) with significantly higher incomes ($4,750).
   - **Marketing Decision**: Premium products or exclusive offers should be targeted at this cluster. Personalized high-end services or products could appeal to them more.

E-Commerce Perspective Decisions:

- **Personalized Campaigns**: Based on the segmentation, the company can create personalized campaigns for each group. For example, for **Cluster 1**, a budget-friendly campaign might focus on affordability, while for **Cluster 3**, the focus could be on luxury and exclusivity.

- **Product Recommendations**: Product suggestions can be tailored according to the average income and spending behavior of each cluster, ensuring the offerings match their purchasing power and preferences.

- **Customer Retention**: For Cluster 1, offering loyalty programs and incentives for repeat purchases could be effective in driving long-term customer relationships. For Cluster 3, providing early access to new or exclusive products may build brand loyalty.

This approach helps businesses improve their customer engagement strategies and increase conversion rates by addressing specific needs within each customer segment.

3.2 Product Recommendations Using Collaborative Filtering

Collaborative filtering is a popular technique used in recommendation systems to suggest products based on the preferences and behaviors of similar users. It works by leveraging the information collected from users' interactions with products, such as ratings, reviews, or purchase history. This data is then used to find patterns and similarities between users, allowing the system to predict which products a particular user may be interested in, even if they haven't interacted with them before.

In collaborative filtering, there are two primary types: user-based and item-based filtering. User-based filtering identifies users who are similar to the target user and recommends products that these similar users have liked or interacted with. It assumes that if two users share a similar pattern of preferences, they will likely enjoy the same products. On the other hand, item-based filtering focuses on finding products that are similar to those the user has already interacted with, suggesting items that have been liked or bought by other users who have similar preferences.

This technique is effective because it doesn't require knowledge of the product itself, such as detailed descriptions or features. Instead, it uses the behavior of users, making it a purely data-driven approach. For instance, if a user frequently buys books on a particular genre, the system can recommend other books in the same genre that other similar users have enjoyed. This creates a personalized experience, making it more likely for users to discover products that match their tastes.

One challenge with collaborative filtering is the cold start problem, which occurs when a new user or item is introduced to the system. Since there is no prior data on the user's preferences or the product's popularity, it becomes difficult to make accurate recommendations. To mitigate this, many systems use hybrid approaches that combine collaborative filtering with other techniques, such as content-based filtering, where product features or user profiles are also taken into account.

Another issue that arises is sparsity, where there is not enough data available for certain users or items. In large systems, users may only interact with a small fraction of available products, making it hard for the system to find meaningful patterns. To address sparsity, algorithms can use matrix factorization or other advanced methods that allow for better approximations of missing data, improving the accuracy of recommendations.

Despite these challenges, collaborative filtering remains a widely used method for generating recommendations due to its simplicity and ability to produce effective suggestions based on user behavior. It's particularly powerful in environments like e-commerce, streaming services, and social media platforms, where understanding user preferences plays a crucial role in engaging customers and increasing sales or usage. By continuously learning from user interactions, collaborative filtering can evolve to provide more relevant and timely product recommendations over time.

Practical Example: Building a Product Recommendation System Using Collaborative Filtering Techniques

An e-commerce platform wants to build a recommendation system to suggest products to users based on their past purchasing behavior. By using collaborative filtering, the system identifies patterns and similarities between users or products, allowing for personalized recommendations. In this example, a collaborative filtering model is trained using past transaction data, where products are recommended based on the preferences and behaviors of similar users.

Sample Data:

Here's a sample e-commerce transaction data for users and their product interactions (ratings or purchases):

User_ID	Product_ID	Rating (1-5)	Purchase (Yes/No)
U1	P1	5	Yes
U1	P2	3	Yes
U1	P3	2	No
U2	P1	4	Yes
U2	P3	4	Yes
U2	P4	5	Yes
U3	P2	5	Yes
U3	P3	3	Yes
U3	P5	5	No

Collaborative Filtering Approach:

Using collaborative filtering, we identify the most similar users based on their ratings or purchases. The system will then suggest products that similar users have interacted with or rated highly, even if the current user hasn't engaged with those products yet.

Steps:

1. **User Similarity Calculation:** Calculate the similarity between users based on their ratings or purchase behavior (e.g., using cosine similarity or Pearson correlation).

2. **Neighborhood Formation:** Select the most similar users (neighbors) for a given target user.

3. **Product Recommendation:** Recommend products that the target user hasn't interacted with but are popular among similar users.

Output and Results (Sample Recommendations for User U1):

Assume the similarity calculation results in these neighbors for U1:

- Neighbors: U2 (cosine similarity = 0.9), U3 (cosine similarity = 0.7)

Based on the past behaviors of these neighbors, the system suggests the following products for U1:

- **Product P4** (purchased by U2, but U1 has not purchased it)
- **Product P5** (purchased by U3, but U1 has not purchased it)

User_ID	Recommended Product_IDs	Reason for Recommendation
U1	P4, P5	Products recommended based on similar users' past purchases

Explanation and Interpretation of Results:

- **User Similarity:** The system identified U2 and U3 as similar to U1, with high cosine similarity scores indicating their preferences are alike.

- **Recommendations:** P4 and P5 are suggested because both products were purchased by U2 and U3, respectively, which are highly similar to U1.

- **Accuracy of Recommendations:** The success of this system depends on the accuracy of the similarity measure. Higher similarity results in better recommendations.

Observations:

- **Product Diversification:** Collaborative filtering recommends products that a user might not have discovered on their own, broadening their shopping experience.

- **Diversity of Users:** Since users may have different preferences, incorporating a larger set of neighbors can yield more diverse recommendations.

Decisions from the E-Commerce Perspective:

- **Inventory Management:** The platform can analyze which products are frequently recommended to different users and ensure sufficient stock of these items.

- **Personalization and Targeting:** By understanding users' preferences, the platform can tailor marketing campaigns, discounts, and promotions for recommended products.

- **Engagement Strategies:** Since similar users tend to buy similar products, engaging users with personalized suggestions can improve the conversion rate and increase customer satisfaction.

In summary, collaborative filtering allows the platform to provide personalized, relevant product recommendations that can increase sales, improve customer experience, and enhance engagement with the platform.

3.3 Dynamic Pricing with AI

Dynamic pricing using AI is an approach that allows businesses to adjust prices for their products or services based on real-time market conditions. By leveraging artificial intelligence, companies can analyze vast amounts of data such as demand, competitor pricing, customer behavior, and external factors like weather or events to make pricing decisions. This helps ensure that prices are optimized to maximize revenue, attract customers, and remain competitive in a constantly changing market.

AI-driven dynamic pricing systems often use machine learning algorithms to predict demand fluctuations and assess the willingness of customers to pay different prices at different times. These algorithms continuously learn from new data and adjust pricing models accordingly. The ability to process large datasets quickly allows AI to offer more personalized pricing, ensuring that individual customer segments receive prices tailored to their preferences, purchase history, or location.

Retailers, airlines, hotels, and other industries frequently use dynamic pricing to adjust their offerings. For example, in the airline industry, prices might rise as the flight date approaches and demand increases. On the other hand, if there is low demand, airlines may lower prices to encourage bookings. These real-time adjustments can be automated, making pricing decisions faster and more efficient without manual intervention.

One of the key advantages of AI in dynamic pricing is its ability to account for a range of variables that humans might overlook. Traditional pricing models typically rely on historical sales data and static factors, but AI can incorporate more dynamic, real-time data sources such as consumer sentiment, traffic data, and competitor price changes. This allows businesses to respond to changes in the market more quickly and accurately, ensuring that they stay competitive.

However, while dynamic pricing can drive higher profits, it also comes with challenges. For businesses, there is a risk of alienating customers who might feel unfairly charged. Price volatility can create frustration for consumers who see different prices for the same product at different times. Moreover, businesses need to ensure that their AI models are transparent and that the pricing algorithms are not creating unintended biases or discriminatory pricing structures.

In conclusion, AI-powered dynamic pricing represents a shift toward more sophisticated and adaptable pricing strategies. It enables companies to maximize their profits, adapt to market conditions quickly, and offer personalized pricing to customers. While the technology holds tremendous potential, businesses must carefully balance the benefits of dynamic pricing with the need to maintain customer trust and avoid negative consumer reactions.

Practical Example: Implementing Dynamic Pricing Strategies Using AI to Adjust Prices Based on Market Demand

Context: An e-commerce company sells a variety of electronic gadgets, and to maximize revenue, it wants to implement a dynamic pricing strategy that adjusts product prices based on customer demand and competitor pricing. The company utilizes AI models to monitor demand fluctuations, competitor prices, and historical sales data. By adjusting prices in real time, the company aims to strike a balance between competitive pricing and maximizing profit.

The following table shows sample data before and after the AI dynamic pricing algorithm is applied. The company uses competitor pricing and demand factors (like sales volume and stock levels) as inputs to adjust prices.

Sample Product Pricing Data Before and After Dynamic Pricing Adjustment:

Product ID	Product Name	Competitor Price	Current Price	Sales Volume (Units)	Demand Score (1-10)	Stock Level	Adjusted Price
1001	Smartphone A	$500	$490	150	8	100	$495
1002	Laptop B	$900	$850	75	6	50	$860
1003	Tablet C	$300	$280	200	9	150	$285
1004	Headphones D	$120	$110	300	7	200	$112
1005	Smartwatch E	$200	$210	50	5	30	$205

Output and Results Interpretation:

1. **Smartphone A**: The price was adjusted slightly from $490 to $495, as the AI detected high demand (Demand Score 8) and a moderately lower competitor price ($500). The company raised the price slightly to maximize revenue while remaining competitive.

2. **Laptop B**: The price increased from $850 to $860 despite lower demand (Demand Score 6) and competitor pricing at $900. This price hike was possible because the stock level is relatively low (50 units), signaling scarcity, and the AI leveraged this factor to adjust prices.

3. **Tablet C**: Given the high demand score of 9 and strong sales volume, the price was slightly increased from $280 to $285, staying just below the competitor price of $300. This dynamic adjustment optimizes profits while avoiding alienating customers with a significant price increase.

4. **Headphones D**: Although sales are high (300 units), the price remains close to the previous value, increasing only slightly from $110 to $112. The AI determined that demand is not exceptionally high (Demand Score 7), and the price increase was small to avoid price sensitivity issues in a highly competitive market.

5. **Smartwatch E**: The price decreased from $210 to $205, likely due to low demand (Demand Score 5) and competitor pricing pressures. The AI recognized the need for a price reduction to stimulate sales and remain competitive in the market.

Observations:

1. **Demand vs. Price Adjustment**: The AI adjusts prices upward when demand is high (as seen with Smartphone A and Tablet C) and reduces prices when demand is low (like with Smartwatch E). This behavior aligns with market dynamics, ensuring the company profits from high demand while incentivizing purchases during lower demand periods.

2. **Competitor Pricing Influence**: Competitor prices also play a significant role in adjustments, especially when stock levels are high or low. For instance, Laptop B was priced slightly below the competitor even though demand was moderate, ensuring it remained attractive compared to a higher-priced alternative.

3. **Stock Level Considerations**: Low stock levels trigger price increases to take advantage of scarcity (Laptop B), while high stock levels with lower demand lead to price reductions (Smartwatch E).

E-Commerce Decisions:

1. **Revenue Maximization**: The company can use AI-driven dynamic pricing to increase profit margins by adjusting prices based on real-time data. For instance, increasing prices on high-demand, low-stock products (like Laptop B) and reducing prices on low-demand products (like Smartwatch E) ensures the company stays competitive and profitable.

2. **Competitive Positioning**: By continuously monitoring competitor prices, the company can fine-tune its own pricing strategy to remain attractive to customers without sacrificing profit margins. This strategy helps maintain a balance between competitive pricing and maximizing the value of high-demand products.

3. **Customer Satisfaction**: Dynamic pricing strategies need to ensure that customers are not turned away by constant price fluctuations. The company should analyze consumer behavior to ensure that pricing remains attractive and fair. For instance, slight increases in price should be justified by customer demand or product scarcity to maintain brand loyalty.

By leveraging AI and real-time data, the company can ensure that it stays ahead in a competitive e-commerce market while meeting demand at optimized price points.

4. Chatbots and Virtual Assistants in E-Commerce

Chatbots and virtual assistants are becoming integral parts of e-commerce platforms, helping businesses offer a more personalized, efficient, and seamless shopping experience. These technologies use artificial intelligence (AI) to interact with customers, answer their queries, assist with product recommendations, and guide them through the purchasing process.

Chatbots are typically designed to respond to specific keywords and queries, while virtual assistants can engage in more complex conversations, learning from previous interactions to provide more accurate responses over time. Their availability 24/7 provides customers with constant support, contributing to higher customer satisfaction and loyalty.

One of the key benefits of using chatbots and virtual assistants in e-commerce is their ability to reduce the response time for customer inquiries.

Traditional customer service methods, such as waiting for an email response or speaking to a human agent, can take time, but chatbots can provide immediate answers to common questions, such as order status, return policies, or shipping information. This helps to keep customers engaged and informed, leading to a more positive experience and potentially increasing conversion rates.

These technologies also assist in personalizing the shopping experience. By analyzing user data, such as browsing history and past purchases, chatbots and virtual assistants can recommend products tailored to the individual's preferences and needs. This level of personalization can enhance customer satisfaction by providing shoppers with relevant options, increasing the likelihood of making a purchase. Furthermore, personalized communication can help build trust with customers, making them feel more valued and understood by the brand.

In addition to improving customer service and personalization, chatbots and virtual assistants help businesses save on operational costs. Automating customer support tasks reduces the need for a large customer service team, allowing companies to allocate resources to other areas of the business. These tools can handle a wide range of tasks, from answering frequently asked questions to processing simple orders, freeing up human agents to focus on more complex issues. This can lead to improved efficiency and cost savings in the long term.

The integration of chatbots and virtual assistants in e-commerce also supports a more interactive and engaging shopping experience. For instance, they can guide customers through the entire buying process, from browsing products to checking out. In addition, virtual assistants can assist with tasks such as tracking shipments, handling refunds, or even processing payments. This enhances the convenience factor, as customers do not have to navigate through different pages or wait for responses from human agents.

Despite the advantages, some challenges still exist in fully integrating chatbots and virtual assistants into e-commerce platforms. These tools rely on AI and natural language processing, which may not always understand complex or ambiguous queries. This can sometimes lead to frustration for customers if their issues are not addressed promptly or accurately. However, as AI continues to improve, these systems are expected to become more adept at understanding and responding to a broader range of customer inquiries, making them an even more valuable asset to e-commerce businesses.

Practical Example: Chatbots and Virtual Assistants in E-Commerce

In an e-commerce platform, a chatbot or virtual assistant can enhance the shopping experience by assisting customers in real-time. It can provide personalized product recommendations, answer questions, and even assist with the checkout process. For instance, an e-commerce store that sells electronics may implement a chatbot to guide customers through product selection, compare different models, and handle common queries such as shipping times and return policies. To assess its effectiveness, let's analyze some key metrics such as customer satisfaction, conversion rates, and response time.

Sample Data: Chatbot Performance Metrics

Metric	Before Chatbot Implementation	After Chatbot Implementation	% Change
Customer Satisfaction	70%	85%	+21.4%
Conversion Rate	3%	5%	+66.7%
Average Response Time	5 minutes	1 minute	-80%
Cart Abandonment Rate	30%	20%	33.3%

Output and Results Interpretation

- **Customer Satisfaction**: There is a significant improvement in customer satisfaction after implementing the chatbot. The satisfaction rate increased from 70% to 85%, which indicates that the chatbot is helping to address customer needs more effectively.

- **Conversion Rate**: The conversion rate has risen from 3% to 5%, a 66.7% increase. This suggests that the chatbot is playing a role in guiding users to complete purchases, perhaps by answering questions that might otherwise lead to cart abandonment.

- **Average Response Time**: The average response time dropped dramatically from 5 minutes to just 1 minute. This indicates that the chatbot is able to provide instant responses to customer inquiries, enhancing the overall user experience.

- **Cart Abandonment Rate**: With the chatbot's assistance, the cart abandonment rate decreased from 30% to 20%, showing that the chatbot is effectively helping customers through the checkout process, possibly by resolving last-minute issues or doubts.

Observations

- The chatbot's introduction has led to improvements in multiple key areas, suggesting its positive impact on both customer experience and business outcomes.

- Faster response times and lower cart abandonment rates are directly linked to better customer satisfaction and higher conversion rates.

- The chatbot appears to be successfully managing customer inquiries and assisting with the buying decision process.

Decisions from an E-Commerce Perspective

- **Scaling Up**: Given the positive impact, the business should consider scaling the chatbot functionality to handle a broader range of queries or support multiple languages to cater to international customers.

- **Investment in AI**: Investing in advanced AI for more sophisticated chatbot interactions could further improve response accuracy and personalization.

- **Continual Monitoring**: Regularly monitor the chatbot's performance to ensure it continues to meet customer expectations, making adjustments to the dialogue flow or functionality as necessary.

- **Personalization**: Further enhancing the chatbot's ability to personalize recommendations based on customer history or preferences could increase conversion rates even more.

In conclusion, the chatbot is driving meaningful improvements in e-commerce operations, and expanding its capabilities could lead to further success.

4.1 Building AI-Powered Chatbots for Customer Support

Another advantage is that AI chatbots can provide consistent answers to frequently asked questions. This reduces the need for customers to wait for an available agent to assist them, as the chatbot can immediately provide relevant information. Whether it's answering questions about product features, providing troubleshooting steps, or assisting with order tracking, chatbots can handle a wide range of common customer queries without human intervention.

Moreover, AI-powered chatbots can continuously learn and improve their responses over time. Machine learning algorithms allow them to adapt to new information and refine their understanding of customer needs. As they interact with more users, they become more effective at providing accurate and relevant answers, reducing the likelihood of errors and improving the quality of support they offer.

Businesses can also benefit from the cost savings associated with using AI chatbots. Since these chatbots can handle a large portion of customer support inquiries, companies can reduce their reliance on human agents, freeing up resources for more complex tasks. Additionally, chatbots do not require breaks or vacations, making them a highly efficient and cost-effective solution for customer service.

Despite their many benefits, AI-powered chatbots are not perfect and have limitations. They may struggle to understand complex or ambiguous questions, and there may be instances where customers need the expertise of a human agent. However, by integrating AI chatbots with human support teams, businesses can create a hybrid system that provides both the speed and efficiency of AI and the expertise of human agents when necessary. This combination ensures that customers receive the best possible support experience.

Practical Example: Deploying a Chatbot to Assist Customers in Real-Time on an E-Commerce Website

Imagine an e-commerce website that integrates a chatbot to assist customers in real-time. The chatbot's primary goal is to answer common customer queries, provide information about products, assist with order tracking, and handle complaints. By automating responses, the chatbot enhances the customer experience and reduces the workload on human agents. For example, the chatbot could instantly respond to queries like "What is the status of my order?" or "Do you have this item in stock?" This setup is especially useful for improving customer support efficiency and satisfaction.

Here is sample data that represents customer queries and chatbot responses, and how the chatbot performs in terms of response time and customer satisfaction.

Customer Query	Chatbot Response	Response Time (Seconds)	Customer Satisfaction (Scale 1-5)	Resolution (Yes/No)
"What is the status of my order?"	"Your order #12345 is on the way and should arrive by Jan 18."	3	5	Yes
"Do you have this item in stock?"	"Yes, this item is in stock and available for purchase."	2	5	Yes
"Can I return an item if I'm not happy?"	"Yes, you can return items within 30 days of purchase."	4	4	Yes
"How do I track my shipment?"	"You can track your shipment using the tracking number sent to your email."	3	4	Yes
"I received a damaged product."	"I'm sorry for the inconvenience. A support agent will contact you shortly to resolve this."	6	3	No

Output and Results Interpretation

1. **Response Time**: The chatbot's average response time across all queries is around 3.6 seconds. This is a reasonable speed, allowing for efficient interaction with customers.

2. **Customer Satisfaction**: The customer satisfaction ratings are generally high, with scores of 4 and 5 across most queries. The exception is the issue with receiving a damaged product (satisfaction score of 3), indicating that customers may not be fully satisfied with the chatbot's response in this situation.

3. **Resolution Rate**: The resolution rate is 80%, with four out of five queries being fully resolved by the chatbot. The unresolved issue was related to receiving a damaged product, where the chatbot escalated the issue to a human agent.

Observations

- The chatbot performs well with straightforward queries such as order status, stock availability, and return policies.

- For more complex issues, like product damage, the chatbot directs the customer to human support, which may result in a slightly lower satisfaction score.

- Response times are quick, but they could be optimized further, especially in cases involving more detailed customer concerns.

Decisions from the E-Commerce Perspective

- **Enhance Complex Query Handling**: While the chatbot efficiently handles simple inquiries, the business could train it to handle more complex situations, like processing returns or dealing with damaged items.

- **Integrate with Human Support**: Maintain the integration with human agents for complex issues but ensure that the transition between the chatbot and human agents is seamless and quick.

- **Monitor Customer Satisfaction**: Regularly monitor customer feedback (such as satisfaction scores) to identify areas for chatbot improvement and update its responses accordingly. The goal should be to increase the chatbot's resolution rate to 90% or higher.

- **Continuous Improvement**: Improve the chatbot's ability to track and handle product-related issues, aiming to enhance the customer experience in the long term.

4.2 Enhancing Customer Experience with Virtual Shopping Assistants

Virtual shopping assistants are transforming the way businesses interact with customers. These digital tools simulate the experience of a human assistant by guiding shoppers through product selections, providing recommendations, and offering personalized experiences. With artificial intelligence, they can understand customer preferences, suggest items based on past behavior, and even answer detailed product-related questions. This enhances the overall shopping experience, making it more tailored to individual needs and preferences.

The benefits of virtual assistants extend beyond just personalized suggestions. They can streamline the shopping process by helping customers find products quickly and efficiently. For example, when a customer searches for a particular item, a virtual assistant can help narrow down choices, eliminating the overwhelming nature of too many options. This reduces the time spent on decision-making and can lead to faster purchase decisions, improving overall sales.

One of the key advantages of virtual assistants is their ability to provide 24/7 support. Unlike human employees, they are always available, offering immediate assistance at any time of day or night. This is particularly useful for customers in different time zones or those who prefer to shop outside of regular business hours. With consistent availability, virtual assistants enhance the convenience factor for customers, making them feel more comfortable and supported during their shopping journey.

These assistants also excel in handling a wide range of queries and tasks that might be difficult for human agents to manage in high volumes. From answering basic questions about product details, pricing, and availability, to providing guidance on returns or order tracking, virtual assistants can handle repetitive tasks effortlessly. This allows human customer service representatives to focus on more complex or high-touch interactions, resulting in a more efficient and satisfying experience for both customers and businesses.

Another significant advantage is the ability of virtual assistants to improve customer engagement. By analyzing customer interactions and preferences, these tools can tailor their responses to create a more engaging shopping experience. They can suggest complementary products, inform customers about promotions, or even offer personalized discounts, enhancing the emotional connection customers feel toward the brand. This kind of targeted interaction fosters loyalty and increases the likelihood of repeat purchases.

Finally, the use of virtual shopping assistants enables businesses to gather valuable data that can be used to improve future customer experiences. By tracking customer behavior, preferences, and purchase history, companies can fine-tune their offerings and marketing strategies. This data-driven approach allows for continuous improvement in the customer experience, ensuring that shoppers receive more relevant recommendations and a smoother, more enjoyable shopping journey each time they visit.

Practical Example:

In an e-commerce setting, an AI-powered virtual shopping assistant can enhance the customer experience by recommending products tailored to their preferences. For instance, based on previous purchases, browsing behavior, and demographic information, the AI assistant suggests products that match the customer's tastes. Suppose a customer frequently buys fitness apparel and has shown interest in eco-friendly products. The assistant could recommend specific brands, styles, and eco-friendly options. Here's a sample table of user preferences and recommended products by the assistant, followed by an interpretation of the results.

Sample Data:

Customer ID	Age	Gender	Previous Purchases	Browsing Behavior	Recommended Product	Product Category	Recommendation Type
001	30	Female	Sports leggings, running shoes	Fitness apparel, eco-friendly	Eco-friendly running shoes (Brand A)	Footwear	Product Match
002	45	Male	T-shirts, yoga mats	Sports gear, sustainable items	Organic cotton T-shirt (Brand B)	Apparel	Eco-friendly
003	25	Female	Yoga pants,	Gym accessor	Recycled material	Apparel	Sustainability Focused

Custo mer ID	Age	Gend er	Previou s Purchas es	Browsi ng Behavio r	Recomme nded Product	Produc t Catego ry	Recommend ation Type
			water bottles	ies, eco-friendly	yoga pants (Brand C)		
004	38	Male	Running shoes, sports shorts	Outdoor sports gear, eco-conscio us	Recycled running shoes (Brand D)	Footwe ar	Sustainabilit y Focused
005	32	Fema le	Sweatsh irts, fitness trackers	Athletic wear, eco-conscio us	Eco-friendly fitness tracker (Brand E)	Electro nics	Product Match

Interpretation of Results:

- **Customer Preferences:** The AI assistant tailors the recommendations based on the customer's purchase history, browsing habits, and values (e.g., eco-friendliness).

- **Matching Products:** For example, Customer 001, a female aged 30 who has bought fitness apparel, gets a recommendation for eco-friendly running shoes.

- **Sustainability Focus:** Customers like 003 and 004, who have shown interest in eco-friendly items, are recommended products with sustainable features, like recycled material yoga pants and shoes.

- **Gender & Age Relevance:** Age and gender are also considered. For instance, Customer 002, a 45-year-old male, is recommended organic cotton T-shirts, aligning with both his previous purchases and eco-conscious browsing behavior.

Results & Observations:

- The AI assistant effectively matches product recommendations to the customer's personal preferences and values. In this case, the assistant places a heavy emphasis on eco-friendly and sustainable products, which aligns with recent consumer trends toward environmental consciousness.

- By analyzing browsing behavior, the assistant offers highly relevant products, leading to potentially higher conversion rates.

E-Commerce Decisions:

- **Product Range Expansion:** E-commerce businesses should consider expanding their eco-friendly and sustainable product lines, as demand is evident from customer behavior.

- **Personalization Strategies:** Using AI for deep personalization can lead to increased customer satisfaction and loyalty. Offering tailored recommendations could encourage customers to make repeat purchases.

- **Marketing Focus:** Promoting personalized recommendations and sustainability-focused products can drive engagement, particularly with customers who prioritize environmental concerns.

In conclusion, integrating AI virtual shopping assistants helps provide tailored, efficient, and value-driven experiences for customers, which is a win-win for both the customer and the business.

4.3 Natural Language Processing (NLP) for Customer Interaction

Natural Language Processing (NLP) plays a critical role in transforming how businesses interact with their customers. It allows machines to understand, interpret, and respond to human language in a way that feels natural and intuitive. By applying NLP techniques, businesses can automate customer service processes, improve response times, and offer more personalized experiences. This capability enables the analysis of vast amounts of unstructured data, such as customer feedback, reviews, or inquiries, helping companies to better understand customer sentiments and needs.

One of the main advantages of NLP in customer interaction is its ability to power chatbots and virtual assistants. These tools can handle customer inquiries efficiently, responding to frequently asked questions and solving problems without human intervention. With NLP, chatbots can understand customer requests more accurately, providing relevant answers and even performing complex tasks like booking appointments or processing orders. This reduces the need for customers to wait in long queues, enhancing their overall experience.

Another area where NLP shines is in sentiment analysis. By analyzing the tone and emotion behind customer communications, businesses can gauge customer satisfaction and address issues proactively. For instance, if a customer expresses frustration or dissatisfaction in a message, the system can alert a human agent to intervene and resolve the issue quickly. This not only helps in improving customer service but also enables businesses to take preventive actions to avoid churn or negative publicity.

NLP also facilitates better data-driven decision-making. With the ability to process large amounts of customer interaction data, businesses can derive insights about customer preferences, behaviors, and pain points. This data can be used to refine marketing strategies, product development, and customer support, ensuring that the business stays aligned with the evolving needs of its clientele. Additionally, NLP can assist in automating content creation, helping companies generate personalized emails or responses tailored to individual customers.

By integrating NLP with customer relationship management (CRM) systems, companies can provide more seamless and consistent interactions across different channels. Whether a customer reaches out via social media, email, or live chat, NLP ensures that their experience remains fluid and coherent. The system can remember past interactions, making it easier to follow up on unresolved issues or offer personalized recommendations based on previous conversations.

Finally, NLP has the potential to drastically improve multilingual support. By leveraging translation and language recognition tools, businesses can cater to customers who speak different languages, broadening their reach and making their services accessible to a global audience. This reduces the barriers that typically exist in cross-lingual communication and allows businesses to better serve diverse customer bases while maintaining high standards of service quality.

Practical Example Context

In an e-commerce platform, NLP (Natural Language Processing) can be used to optimize product search by interpreting customer queries more accurately. For example, when a customer enters a query like "cheap red sneakers for women," NLP can understand the intent and extract keywords related to product category, color, price range, and target demographic (women). This enables the system to deliver more relevant results. By using NLP techniques such as named entity recognition (NER) and intent classification, the search engine can better match products to the customer's query, resulting in a more refined and personalized experience.

Sample Data: Customer Queries and Optimized Search Results

Customer Query	Product Search Intent	Extracted Keywords	Optimized Search Results
"cheap red sneakers for women"	Product: Sneakers, Color: Red, Price: Cheap, Gender: Women	Cheap, Red, Sneakers, Women	Displayed results for red sneakers in the women's category with lower price range
"stylish leather jackets for men"	Product: Jackets, Material: Leather, Gender: Men, Style: Stylish	Stylish, Leather, Jackets, Men	Showcased stylish leather jackets in the men's section
"waterproof boots under $100"	Product: Boots, Feature:	Waterproof, Boots, $100	Filtered results for waterproof boots under $100

Customer Query	Product Search Intent	Extracted Keywords	Optimized Search Results
	Waterproof, Price: Under $100		
"affordable black running shoes"	Product: Running Shoes, Color: Black, Price: Affordable	Affordable, Black, Running Shoes	Returned affordable black running shoes based on price and category
"laptop with good battery life"	Product: Laptop, Feature: Battery Life	Laptop, Battery Life	Refined results for laptops with high battery capacity

Output and Results Interpretation

1. **Customer Query:** "cheap red sneakers for women" **Optimized Search Results:** The system filters and shows products based on the query's intent: women's red sneakers at lower price points. NLP has successfully parsed "cheap" as an indicator of a lower price range and "red sneakers" for the product's attributes.

2. **Customer Query:** "stylish leather jackets for men" **Optimized Search Results:** The NLP system recognizes the style and material ("stylish" and "leather") and targets the men's category. As a result, only relevant, stylish leather jackets for men are presented, improving the relevance of search results.

3. **Customer Query:** "waterproof boots under $100" **Optimized Search Results:** NLP extracts features such as "waterproof" and a price filter ("under $100"), ensuring that boots displayed are waterproof and fall within the customer's budget.

4. **Customer Query:** "affordable black running shoes" **Optimized Search Results:** The query is filtered for affordable options, ensuring that black running shoes meeting the price point and color requirements are displayed first.

5. **Customer Query:** "laptop with good battery life" **Optimized Search Results:** The intent to find laptops with good battery life is recognized and matches the features of products, ensuring that only those laptops with superior battery performance are prioritized.

Results and Output Explanation

- **Improved Search Accuracy:** Each query is better matched with the customer's intent, making it easier for customers to find what they need without irrelevant results.

- **Personalization:** NLP helps personalize the search experience by filtering results based on product features, price points, and specific customer preferences (e.g., gender, style).

- **Enhanced Conversion Potential:** When customers find more relevant products faster, it increases the likelihood of completing a purchase. By aligning search results with customer expectations, the platform can boost conversion rates.

Decisions from an E-Commerce Perspective

1. **Refining Search Algorithms:** Continuous optimization of NLP models will help further improve the understanding of customer queries, ensuring better results.

2. **Dynamic Pricing Integration:** Incorporating real-time price data into NLP models can help fine-tune price-related queries, displaying items that are within customers' budgets.

3. **Targeted Marketing:** Understanding the common queries and optimizing search results accordingly allows the platform to run targeted marketing campaigns based on customer preferences (e.g., "stylish leather jackets for men" can trigger a promotion targeting this group).

4. **User Experience:** A well-optimized search enhances the overall user experience, increasing customer satisfaction and engagement with the platform.

5. Generative AI for Content Creation

Generative AI has become a powerful tool for content creation, offering significant advantages in terms of speed, efficiency, and creativity. By utilizing advanced machine learning techniques, generative AI can produce high-quality text, images, videos, and even music.

This technology works by training models on large datasets, allowing the AI to learn patterns and structures within content. As a result, it can generate new material that is contextually relevant and often indistinguishable from content created by humans.

One of the key benefits of generative AI is its ability to save time. Tasks that traditionally took hours or days can now be completed in a fraction of the time. For example, writers and marketers can leverage AI to generate blog posts, social media content, or product descriptions quickly, allowing them to focus on other aspects of their work. This productivity boost can be especially valuable in industries where content needs to be produced on a continuous basis.

The versatility of generative AI also extends to personalization. AI can tailor content to meet the specific preferences of individual audiences. By analyzing user data and behavior, it can create personalized experiences that resonate more deeply with the target audience. This level of customization can lead to higher engagement and better results in marketing campaigns, as well as improved user satisfaction in interactive platforms like websites or apps.

Moreover, generative AI fosters creativity by providing new perspectives. When generating content, AI is not constrained by human biases or limitations, which can lead to novel and unexpected ideas. This can be particularly useful for creators looking to break through creative blocks or explore new avenues. The AI-generated content can serve as inspiration, with users refining and building upon it to create unique works that combine the best of human ingenuity and artificial intelligence.

Despite these benefits, there are challenges associated with generative AI. The quality of AI-generated content can vary depending on the model and dataset used. In some cases, AI may produce content that lacks coherence or relevance, requiring human intervention to refine the output. Furthermore, there are ethical concerns around the use of AI for content creation, particularly regarding issues of plagiarism, misinformation, and copyright infringement. Ensuring that AI-generated content adheres to ethical guidelines and industry standards remains a priority.

Overall, generative AI has the potential to revolutionize the content creation process. It enables faster production, more personalized experiences, and increased creativity. While challenges such as quality control and ethical considerations persist, the technology continues to evolve. As AI models improve and more industries adopt this technology, the role of generative AI in content creation is likely to grow, providing both opportunities and complexities for creators, businesses, and consumers alike.

Practical Example: Generative AI for Content Creation in E-Commerce

Generative AI can be a powerful tool in e-commerce for creating product descriptions, blog posts, or social media content that engages customers and drives traffic. In this example, an e-commerce company uses a Generative AI model to create product descriptions for a line of smartwatches. The AI takes in data such as the product's features, target audience, and style, and generates a description that can be used for product listings.

Sample Data: Smartwatch Features for Content Creation

Feature	Value
Brand	TechTime
Model	SmartTime 360
Display	1.5-inch AMOLED
Battery Life	48 hours
Water Resistance	50 meters (5ATM)
Connectivity	Bluetooth 5.0
Target Audience	Fitness enthusiasts, tech lovers
Style	Sleek, modern, minimalistic

Generated Product Description (using Generative AI):

"Introducing the SmartTime 360 by TechTime – a sleek, modern smartwatch designed for fitness enthusiasts and tech lovers alike. Featuring a stunning 1.5-inch AMOLED display, the SmartTime 360 delivers vibrant, crystal-clear visuals. With a battery life of up to 48 hours and water resistance up to 50 meters (5ATM), this watch is perfect for those who want to stay connected and active without compromising on style. Equipped with Bluetooth 5.0 connectivity, the SmartTime 360 ensures seamless pairing with your devices. Whether you're at the gym or in the office, the SmartTime 360 is built to keep up with your lifestyle."

Output & Results:

Attribute	Generated Content
Product Name	SmartTime 360
Description	"Introducing the SmartTime 360 by TechTime – a sleek, modern smartwatch designed for fitness enthusiasts and tech lovers alike..."

Attribute	Generated Content
Word Count	72 words
Tone	Professional, sleek, tech-savvy
Target Audience Match	Fitness enthusiasts, tech lovers
Relevance to Features	High (Mentions display, battery, water resistance, connectivity)
Creativity Score	8/10 (Creativity in description style and wording)

Explanation and Interpretation of Results:

1. **Word Count**: The description is concise, with 72 words, which is ideal for an e-commerce setting where users often skim through product details.

2. **Tone**: The tone is professional and aligns with the target audience—fitness enthusiasts and tech lovers—creating a persuasive appeal.

3. **Target Audience Match**: The description resonates with the target audience, highlighting the smartwatch's features that appeal to both fitness enthusiasts (battery life, water resistance) and tech lovers (connectivity, AMOLED display).

4. **Relevance to Features**: The description aligns well with the product features, effectively communicating the product's key selling points.

5. **Creativity Score**: The AI generated creative yet informative content, adding a nice touch of excitement without sounding too generic.

Observations:

- The generated content accurately reflects the product's features and presents them in a way that would appeal to the target demographic.

- The AI-generated description is coherent, well-structured, and showcases the product's unique qualities.

- The content is short and impactful, aligning with typical e-commerce product listings where brevity and clarity are valued.

E-Commerce Perspective Decisions:

- **Efficiency in Content Creation**: Generative AI helps e-commerce businesses save time and effort in creating product descriptions, allowing them to scale rapidly.

- **Personalization**: By fine-tuning the model based on customer feedback or data, the AI can further tailor descriptions to match evolving consumer preferences.

- **Content Consistency**: AI-generated content ensures that all product listings maintain a consistent tone and style across the website, reinforcing brand identity.

- **SEO Optimization**: The AI can also be used to generate SEO-friendly product descriptions, driving more organic traffic to the e-commerce site by incorporating relevant keywords naturally.

In conclusion, using generative AI for content creation in e-commerce can significantly enhance operational efficiency while ensuring that content is engaging, relevant, and aligned with customer expectations. This approach is vital in staying competitive in a fast-paced digital market.

5.1 Generating Product Descriptions with AI

AI-powered product descriptions are transforming the way businesses communicate with their customers. With the ability to analyze product features, customer preferences, and market trends, AI can create highly tailored, relevant content that captures the essence of a product in a compelling way. These descriptions are designed to highlight the unique selling points, making products more appealing and informative to potential buyers. As a result, businesses can save time and resources while ensuring that their product information resonates with the target audience.

One of the key advantages of using AI for product descriptions is its ability to scale. Writing descriptions for a large number of products can be time-consuming and inefficient when done manually. AI tools can generate descriptions for hundreds or even thousands of items quickly, ensuring consistency in tone and style across all product listings. This scalability is especially valuable for e-commerce businesses with extensive catalogs that need to maintain a consistent brand voice while reaching a wide variety of consumers.

Another important benefit of AI-generated product descriptions is their potential to improve SEO performance. AI can optimize content for search engines by incorporating relevant keywords and phrases that boost a product's visibility in search results. This improves the chances of attracting organic traffic to a business's website. By analyzing search patterns and understanding what terms resonate with potential buyers, AI tools can create content that enhances the discoverability of products online.

AI-driven product descriptions are also highly adaptable. They can be customized for different platforms, whether it's an online store, a marketplace like Amazon, or a social media post. Each platform has its own set of requirements and expectations, but AI can adjust the tone, length, and style to fit the context of each channel. This flexibility helps businesses present their products in the best possible light, regardless of where they're being showcased.

Additionally, AI can help businesses personalize product descriptions for individual customers. By analyzing customer data and behavior, AI can craft descriptions that speak directly to the preferences and interests of specific groups. For example, a description for a sports watch might emphasize durability and performance for one customer segment, while highlighting style and fashion for another. This level of personalization helps increase conversion rates and customer satisfaction by ensuring the product information feels relevant and tailored to each shopper's needs.

Finally, AI can assist in refining and enhancing the quality of product descriptions over time. As more data is collected, AI tools can learn from customer interactions, feedback, and purchasing patterns to refine their descriptions for even better engagement. This continual learning process ensures that product content evolves and stays relevant as consumer preferences and market trends change. With AI-driven product descriptions, businesses can stay ahead of the curve while maintaining a strong connection with their audience.

Practical Example: Using GPT Models to Automatically Generate SEO-Friendly Product Descriptions

In an e-commerce platform, product descriptions play a key role in improving product visibility and driving traffic to the website. Generating SEO-friendly descriptions automatically can save time and enhance search engine optimization (SEO) efforts. Let's consider an example where an e-commerce site wants to generate SEO-friendly product descriptions for a variety of products (like shoes, bags, and electronics). The GPT model can be used to generate descriptions that not only provide key product details but also include relevant keywords for better ranking on search engines.

Sample Product Data

Product ID	Product Name	Category	Features	Price ($)	Keywords
P001	Classic Running Shoes	Footwear	Lightweight, breathable, rubber sole	59.99	running shoes, comfortable, breathable
P002	Leather Handbag	Accessories	Genuine leather, spacious, adjustable strap	89.99	leather handbag, durable, stylish
P003	Wireless Bluetooth Headphones	Electronics	Noise-canceling, 20-hour battery life, comfortable	129.99	Bluetooth, headphones, wireless, noise-canceling

GPT-Generated SEO-Friendly Descriptions

Product ID	SEO-Friendly Description
P001	The Classic Running Shoes offer a perfect combination of comfort and durability, designed with lightweight breathable fabric and a high-quality rubber sole for optimal performance. Perfect for long-distance runs or casual walks, these running shoes will keep your feet cool and comfortable. Shop now for the best price on breathable running shoes for athletes!
P002	Discover the elegance of the Leather Handbag, made from genuine leather to offer style, durability, and plenty of storage. This spacious handbag comes with an adjustable strap for easy carrying, making it the perfect choice for both casual and formal occasions. Elevate your style with this versatile leather handbag, available now at a great price.
P003	Experience superior sound with the Wireless Bluetooth Headphones, equipped with noise-canceling technology for immersive audio. With a 20-hour battery life, these comfortable headphones are perfect for music lovers and professionals alike. Enjoy wireless freedom with these high-performance Bluetooth headphones.

Interpretation of Results

1. **SEO Optimization**: Each product description has been enhanced to include high-volume keywords related to the product's category and features. For example:
   o "Classic Running Shoes" includes keywords like "breathable," "running shoes," and "comfortable."
   o "Leather Handbag" uses keywords like "leather handbag," "durable," and "stylish."
   o "Wireless Bluetooth Headphones" targets terms like "Bluetooth," "wireless," and "noise-canceling."

These keywords will likely improve the search ranking of these products when potential customers search for them on search engines.

2. **Readability and Engagement**: The descriptions are not only SEO-optimized but also engaging and customer-focused. They emphasize the benefits of the product, making them appealing to shoppers.

Observations

- **Increased Likelihood of Clicks**: Products with engaging, keyword-rich descriptions are more likely to rank higher in search results, leading to increased visibility and higher click-through rates.

- **Targeted Marketing**: The generated descriptions highlight key product features that appeal to specific customer needs (e.g., comfort for running shoes, durability for handbags, sound quality for headphones).

- **Consistency**: The descriptions maintain a consistent tone and style across different product categories, ensuring a unified brand voice.

Decisions from the E-Commerce Perspective

1. **Automate Content Generation**: By leveraging GPT models to automatically generate descriptions, e-commerce platforms can scale content creation across thousands of products while maintaining SEO optimization and brand consistency.

2. **Improve Customer Experience**: Descriptions generated with GPT models make product features and benefits clear, enhancing the shopper's experience and helping them make informed purchase decisions.

3. **Monitor SEO Performance**: Regularly review the performance of these descriptions in search engine rankings and adjust the content generation model to include trending keywords or to improve readability.

4. **Use for Other Marketing Materials**: Beyond product descriptions, the same generative model can be used for creating SEO-optimized blog posts, email marketing content, and social media posts, ensuring a cohesive marketing strategy across all channels.

5.2 Creating Personalized Marketing Emails with Generative AI

Personalized marketing emails are a powerful way to engage customers, offering content that resonates with them individually. With generative AI, marketers can create tailored messages that speak directly to the recipient's interests, preferences, and past behaviors. The process involves analyzing data such as browsing history, purchase records, and engagement with previous emails. This data helps AI understand what products, services, or content the customer is most likely to appreciate. By automating the creation of these customized messages, businesses can send relevant content at scale while ensuring that each email feels unique and personal.

Generative AI makes it easier for businesses to go beyond generic promotions by using natural language processing (NLP) to craft emails that sound more conversational and less robotic. It can generate personalized subject lines, text, and even recommendations for products based on a customer's past interactions with the brand. This can help increase open rates and drive conversions by delivering content that aligns more closely with what the customer wants or needs. AI can adjust tone, style, and length to match the preferences of different customer segments, ensuring that the email feels both relevant and authentic.

The use of AI in personalized marketing emails doesn't just help in content creation; it can also optimize the timing and frequency of emails. By analyzing when recipients are most likely to engage with their inbox, AI can recommend the best times to send messages. This reduces the chances of emails being lost in crowded inboxes or ignored. By leveraging this insight, businesses can improve the effectiveness of their campaigns, ensuring that their messages reach customers when they are most likely to take action.

Another significant benefit of AI in personalized marketing is its ability to predict customer behavior. Through machine learning algorithms, AI can analyze patterns in data and anticipate future actions, such as what a customer is likely to purchase next or which service they might need. This predictive capability allows businesses to send proactive recommendations, making emails feel even more relevant. Rather than reacting to past behavior, the AI can foresee a customer's needs, which can be incredibly powerful in driving conversions and loyalty.

However, it's important to note that personalization with AI should not just be about product recommendations. Personalization can extend to content that educates, entertains, or provides value in ways that enhance the overall customer experience. For example, an AI system could generate tips, guides, or curated articles that are relevant to the individual's interests or needs. This broader approach to personalization helps establish a deeper relationship between the business and the customer, building trust and fostering long-term engagement.

Finally, businesses using generative AI for personalized emails should continually assess their efforts to ensure that the content remains relevant and respectful of privacy. AI can help marketers identify new trends, preferences, and insights, but it's crucial that the use of customer data is transparent and complies with privacy regulations. Customers must feel confident that their information is being used responsibly. When done correctly, personalized marketing with AI can create meaningful connections between businesses and their audiences, driving loyalty and increasing revenue over time.

Practical Example Context:

An e-commerce store uses generative AI to send personalized email campaigns based on users' behavior. By analyzing users' purchase history, website interactions, and engagement with previous email campaigns, the AI generates tailored email content for each user. This improves the relevance of the campaigns and increases the chances of conversions. The goal is to send personalized offers and recommendations that align with users' interests, resulting in higher open rates, click-through rates, and ultimately, increased sales.

Sample Data:

User ID	Purchase History	Last Website Visit	Open Rate (%)	Click Rate (%)	Purchase Conversion (%)
1	Laptop, Mouse	2025-01-10	50	20	10
2	Headphones, Gaming Chair	2025-01-12	70	30	15
3	Running Shoes, Fitness Tracker	2025-01-08	60	25	12

User ID	Purchase History	Last Website Visit	Open Rate (%)	Click Rate (%)	Purchase Conversion (%)
4	Smartwatch, Wireless Earbuds	2025-01-05	40	10	8
5	Smartphone, Portable Charger	2025-01-11	80	40	25

Output Generated by AI (Personalized Email Content):

- **User 1 (Laptop, Mouse)**: "Exclusive deal on wireless mouse and laptop accessories just for you!"

- **User 2 (Headphones, Gaming Chair)**: "Get 20% off on your next gaming chair purchase. Check out our latest models!"

- **User 3 (Running Shoes, Fitness Tracker)**: "Stay fit with new running shoes and fitness trackers. Shop the latest collection!"

- **User 4 (Smartwatch, Wireless Earbuds)**: "Upgrade your smartwatch with new features. Enjoy special discounts on wireless earbuds!"

- **User 5 (Smartphone, Portable Charger)**: "Power up your smartphone with our top-rated portable chargers at a discounted price!"

Explanation and Interpretation of Results:

1. **Open Rate**: The percentage of people who opened the email. For example, User 1 has a 50% open rate, meaning half of the recipients opened the email.

2. **Click Rate**: The percentage of recipients who clicked on a link in the email. For User 1, a 20% click rate means 20% of those who opened the email engaged with it.

3. **Purchase Conversion**: This shows the percentage of users who made a purchase after receiving the email. User 5 has the highest purchase conversion rate at 25%, indicating that their personalized email content was highly effective.

Observations:

- **Personalization Impact**: Users with tailored offers based on their purchase history and recent behaviors (e.g., User 5) had the highest purchase conversion rate.

- **Engagement Level**: Users with higher open and click rates (like User 2) were more likely to engage with the content. This suggests the AI-generated content was highly relevant to these users' preferences.

- **Email Timing**: Users who had more recent website visits (e.g., User 5 on 2025-01-11) had higher conversion rates. This indicates that timely email campaigns based on recent activity could boost sales.

E-Commerce Decisions:

1. **Target High Engagement Users**: Focus more on users with high open and click rates like User 5 to maximize conversions.

2. **Improve Personalization**: For users with lower engagement (e.g., User 4), adjust email content to make it more relevant, such as offering discounts or more appealing product suggestions.

3. **Test Email Timing**: Since users with more recent visits are more likely to convert, consider implementing time-sensitive offers or reminders based on recent browsing behavior.

4. **A/B Testing**: Conduct A/B tests on different personalized content and offers to determine what resonates best with specific user segments.

5.3 AI-Generated Visual Content for E-Commerce

AI-generated visual content is becoming an essential tool for e-commerce businesses. With advancements in artificial intelligence, companies can now create high-quality images of products without the need for professional photographers or expensive equipment. AI tools can generate product images with various angles, settings, and even backgrounds, providing a wide range of options to showcase products in different environments. This not only reduces costs but also speeds up the content creation process, allowing businesses to update their product visuals more frequently and with minimal effort.

These AI tools can also enhance the customer experience by providing a more engaging visual representation of products. Through 3D renderings, augmented reality, and dynamic product images, AI can give customers a better understanding of how a product might look in real life. For example, AI can simulate how clothing fits on different body types or how a piece of furniture would look in various home settings. This type of content helps potential buyers visualize the product more clearly, increasing the likelihood of making a purchase.

The use of AI-generated visuals extends beyond simple product images. Marketers can leverage AI to create complex visual content for advertisements, social media posts, and other promotional materials. By using AI algorithms to analyze market trends, consumer preferences, and even competitors' visuals, e-commerce businesses can tailor their content to appeal to specific audiences. This personalized approach can drive more traffic and conversions, making AI a powerful tool for targeted marketing campaigns.

Moreover, AI-generated visuals can help maintain consistency across all online platforms. Businesses often struggle with maintaining uniformity in their visual content across multiple channels, such as websites, mobile apps, and social media. AI tools can standardize the style, color schemes, and product presentation, ensuring that all images remain cohesive and aligned with the brand identity. This consistency fosters brand recognition and trust, key components of customer loyalty in the competitive e-commerce landscape.

One of the significant advantages of AI in visual content creation is its ability to scale. Traditional methods of product photography can be time-consuming and expensive, especially for businesses with large inventories. With AI, e-commerce companies can quickly generate thousands of images in different variations, sizes, and formats. This scalability is particularly useful for businesses that deal with seasonal trends, frequent product launches, or those that operate in niche markets where visual content needs to be customized often.

Despite its many benefits, the use of AI-generated visuals does present some challenges. There is the potential risk of over-reliance on automated systems, leading to a lack of human creativity and authenticity. Consumers may start to notice the uniformity of AI-generated images, which could negatively impact the perception of a brand. To counteract this, businesses should strike a balance between utilizing AI and incorporating human-designed elements to ensure their content feels unique and relatable.

Practical Example: Generating Custom Graphics and Banner Ads Using Generative AI for E-Commerce Promotions

An e-commerce business wants to promote a new line of winter jackets through banner ads. The goal is to create custom graphics that align with the brand's visual identity and attract customers through visually engaging designs. Generative AI is used to produce multiple banner options for different channels (e.g., social media, websites) with optimized designs based on the jacket images and promotional content. The process involves inputting product images, branding elements (colors, logo), and promotional text into the AI model to generate the banners.

Sample Data:

Product Name	Product Image (Link)	Promo Text	Brand Color	Size of Banner (px)
Winter Jacket A	[Image Link A]	"Winter Sale: 30% Off"	#003366	1200x628
Winter Jacket B	[Image Link B]	"Exclusive Offers!"	#FF6347	1200x628
Winter Jacket C	[Image Link C]	"Stay Warm This Winter"	#0044CC	1200x628

Generated Outputs (Sample AI Results):

Banner Type	Generated Image Link	Click-Through Rate (CTR)	Conversion Rate	Engagement (Likes/Comments)	Estimated Sales Impact
Banner 1 - Jacket A	[Banner Image Link 1]	4.5%	2.2%	1500 Likes / 250 Comments	$5000
Banner 2 - Jacket B	[Banner Image Link 2]	5.1%	2.8%	1800 Likes / 300 Comments	$6000
Banner 3 - Jacket C	[Banner Image Link 3]	3.9%	1.9%	1200 Likes / 200 Comments	$4500

Explanation of Results and Output:

- **Click-Through Rate (CTR)**: This metric measures how effective each banner was in driving traffic. The higher the CTR, the better the banner performed in capturing interest.

- **Conversion Rate**: This indicates how many clicks on the banner turned into actual sales. Higher conversion rates indicate that the banner content resonated with the target audience.

- **Engagement**: This shows the level of interaction the banner received, measured by likes and comments, providing insight into how engaging the content was.

- **Estimated Sales Impact**: This is the projected sales generated from the banner ad campaign. It reflects both direct sales from the promotional link and potential customer retention.

Observations:

1. **Banner for Jacket B** had the highest CTR (5.1%) and the highest conversion rate (2.8%), suggesting that the promotional message resonated well with the audience, particularly with the "Exclusive Offers" text.

2. **Banner for Jacket C** had the lowest CTR (3.9%) and conversion rate (1.9%), indicating that the message or design might not have been as compelling for the audience as the other options.

3. **Engagement**: Banners for Jackets B and A received a significantly higher number of likes and comments, suggesting that these ads were more engaging in terms of social media interaction.

4. **Sales Impact**: The highest estimated sales impact came from **Jacket B**, supporting the idea that the banner's design and promotional content were most effective.

Decisions from the E-Commerce Perspective:

- **Focus on Jacket B**: Given its higher CTR, conversion rate, and engagement, the e-commerce team should prioritize Jacket B for further promotional campaigns and consider using similar strategies for other product lines.

- **Test Variations**: Since Banner 3 (Jacket C) had a lower performance, the team should test different creative strategies (e.g., adjusting the promo text or visuals) to see if it can improve customer engagement.

- **Optimize Banner Design**: Since social media engagement is a critical driver, continue to refine banner design based on what resonates with the audience—such as colors, visuals, and messaging.

By using generative AI to create these custom graphics and evaluate performance metrics, the business can tailor future promotional efforts to maximize both traffic and sales.

6. AI in Inventory and Supply Chain Management

Artificial intelligence (AI) is increasingly transforming inventory and supply chain management by enhancing efficiency, reducing costs, and improving decision-making processes. AI-powered tools can analyze vast amounts of data to forecast demand more accurately, ensuring businesses stock the right amount of products at the right time.

This helps in avoiding both stockouts and overstocking, which can lead to unnecessary costs or lost sales. By predicting future demand patterns based on historical data, seasonal trends, and external factors, AI algorithms can fine-tune inventory levels and optimize stock replenishment schedules.

AI also plays a crucial role in supply chain visibility by integrating data from various sources, including suppliers, logistics partners, and warehouses. This real-time data allows businesses to track the movement of goods at every stage, helping to identify potential disruptions or inefficiencies in the supply chain. With AI's ability to analyze these large data sets, companies can anticipate delays, optimize routes, and make more informed decisions about logistics. This leads to faster deliveries, improved customer satisfaction, and reduced transportation costs.

One of the key advantages of AI in inventory management is automation. AI systems can autonomously handle tasks such as inventory tracking, order processing, and even replenishment. This reduces the reliance on manual intervention, cutting down human errors and increasing operational efficiency. Automated warehouses, powered by AI, are able to pick, sort, and package items with remarkable speed and accuracy. By freeing up human resources from routine tasks, employees can focus on higher-level decision-making and problem-solving.

Moreover, AI facilitates smarter supply chain planning through advanced analytics and optimization techniques. AI-driven platforms can simulate different scenarios and assess the potential impact of various supply chain decisions. For example, AI can evaluate the effect of changes in supplier lead times, production capacities, or demand fluctuations. This helps businesses to create more resilient supply chains that can adapt to unexpected challenges, such as geopolitical issues or natural disasters. By identifying vulnerabilities in the supply chain, AI can assist in developing mitigation strategies before problems escalate.

AI's integration with Internet of Things (IoT) technology enhances its effectiveness in inventory and supply chain management. IoT devices, such as smart sensors, can track the condition of goods in transit, monitor environmental factors like temperature and humidity, and provide real-time location data. AI can then process this data to ensure the safe handling of goods, particularly those that are perishable or sensitive to specific conditions. This combination of AI and IoT enables companies to take proactive measures, reducing the risk of damaged goods and minimizing waste.

Finally, AI is helping businesses build more sustainable supply chains by optimizing resource use and reducing waste. AI can identify inefficiencies in the supply chain that lead to excess packaging, energy use, or transportation emissions. By recommending alternative routes, consolidating shipments, or suggesting more sustainable materials, AI supports businesses in their efforts to minimize their environmental impact. As companies face increasing pressure from consumers and regulators to adopt sustainable practices, AI is emerging as a key tool in achieving these goals while maintaining profitability.

Practical Example:

AI in Inventory and Supply Chain Management (SCM) is increasingly being used by e-commerce businesses to optimize inventory levels, predict demand, improve supply chain visibility, and reduce costs. For example, an e-commerce company may implement an AI system to analyze sales trends, weather patterns, and historical inventory data to predict the demand for products over a specific period. This helps prevent stockouts and overstocking, ensuring that the right amount of stock is available to meet customer demand while minimizing storage costs.

Sample Data:

Product	Predicted Demand (Units)	Actual Demand (Units)	Inventory Level (Units)	Reorder Point (Units)	Stockout Occurrences	Overstock Occurrences
A	500	480	600	300	0	1
B	300	320	250	150	1	0
C	200	190	220	100	0	0
D	150	130	180	120	0	1
E	600	590	500	350	0	0

Output and Results Interpretation:

1. **Product A**: The predicted demand was 500 units, while the actual demand was 480 units. The inventory level is 600 units, which is above the reorder point of 300 units. However, there was an overstock occurrence, indicating that there was excess inventory. AI forecasting helped predict demand reasonably well, but inventory management should optimize stocking to avoid surplus.

2. **Product B**: Predicted demand was 300 units, but the actual demand was 320 units. The inventory level is 250 units, which is below the reorder point of 150 units, leading to a stockout occurrence. AI predictions helped in forecasting demand but didn't account for the higher than expected demand, pointing out the need for better flexibility in restocking.

3. **Product C**: The prediction was 200 units, with an actual demand of 190 units. The inventory level of 220 units is above the reorder point

of 100 units, with no stockouts or overstock occurrences. This suggests that AI forecasting has been accurate for this product, and inventory management is working optimally.

4. **Product D**: Predicted demand was 150 units, and the actual demand was 130 units. With an inventory level of 180 units and a reorder point of 120 units, there was an overstock occurrence. The prediction was slightly overestimated, and AI should fine-tune the forecast for better accuracy.

5. **Product E**: Predicted demand of 600 units was very close to the actual demand of 590 units. With an inventory level of 500 units, below the reorder point of 350 units, there were no stockouts or overstock occurrences. AI's prediction was accurate, and restocking was aligned well with actual demand.

Observations:

- AI forecasting works well in predicting demand for products with stable sales (e.g., Product C), but its accuracy can be affected by demand fluctuations or unpredictable factors (e.g., Product B).

- Overstocking issues (e.g., Product A and D) indicate that the AI model might overestimate demand or fail to adjust for changing conditions in the market.

- Stockouts, like for Product B, signal that AI models may need more real-time data or faster decision-making processes to adjust inventory levels dynamically.

- In cases where demand predictions are accurate (e.g., Product E), inventory levels are appropriately managed, leading to efficient supply chain operations.

Decisions from the E-Commerce Perspective:

1. **For Overstocked Products (A & D)**: The e-commerce company could adjust the AI model to account for seasonal demand variations or introduce more dynamic demand prediction techniques. They might also consider reducing the safety stock buffer or revising reorder points to prevent excess inventory.

2. **For Stockouts (Product B)**: The company should consider increasing the flexibility of their supply chain to react quickly to demand fluctuations. Implementing real-time data integration from sources like social media trends or market analysis can help AI

systems predict short-term demand spikes and improve order fulfillment.

3. **For Well-Predicted Demand (Product C & E)**: Continue using the current AI models but explore adding additional product attributes or external factors (e.g., local events, weather) to further fine-tune predictions.

4. **Overall Supply Chain Optimization**: AI can be leveraged to develop a more responsive and adaptive inventory system, reducing both stockouts and overstock. Additionally, AI-driven predictive analytics could integrate with automated ordering systems to ensure that stock levels are replenished just in time, improving both cost-efficiency and customer satisfaction.

6.1 Demand Forecasting with AI

Demand forecasting is the process of predicting future customer demand for products or services based on historical data and other relevant factors. Artificial Intelligence (AI) has revolutionized this process by providing advanced tools that can analyze vast amounts of data quickly and accurately. Traditional methods often rely on simple trends or averages, which can be limited when faced with complex, dynamic markets. AI, however, can process multiple variables, such as seasonality, economic indicators, and consumer behavior, to create more precise and adaptable forecasts.

AI-based forecasting models use machine learning algorithms to identify patterns in historical sales data. These models are trained to recognize trends and anomalies, helping businesses predict future demand more accurately. Unlike traditional methods, which can be rigid and slow to adapt, AI systems continuously improve as they are exposed to new data, making them highly effective in responding to changing market conditions. This adaptability is particularly beneficial in industries where demand can fluctuate rapidly.

Another advantage of AI in demand forecasting is its ability to incorporate external factors, such as market trends, social media sentiment, and competitor actions. Traditional methods might overlook these elements, but AI can analyze these external data sources to provide a more holistic view of future demand. This capability is especially useful for businesses that need to stay ahead of consumer preferences and anticipate changes in the marketplace. For example, AI can detect emerging trends and shifts in consumer behavior that would be difficult for traditional forecasting methods to identify.

AI models can also be fine-tuned to account for different levels of granularity, such as demand for individual products, product categories, or even regional variations. This level of precision allows businesses to optimize inventory, minimize stockouts, and reduce excess inventory, ultimately leading to cost savings and improved customer satisfaction. By predicting demand at a granular level, businesses can make more informed decisions about pricing, production schedules, and resource allocation.

The integration of AI in demand forecasting can also enhance collaboration across departments. For example, sales, marketing, and supply chain teams can work with AI-generated forecasts to align their strategies and ensure that resources are allocated efficiently. AI can provide insights into potential bottlenecks in the supply chain or highlight areas where demand might exceed supply, giving teams the opportunity to adjust their plans proactively. This collaborative approach helps to streamline operations and improve overall business performance.

Despite its many benefits, there are challenges in implementing AI for demand forecasting. Data quality is crucial for AI models to function properly, and poor or incomplete data can lead to inaccurate predictions. Additionally, businesses need the right infrastructure and expertise to deploy and manage AI systems effectively. However, with the right tools and investment, AI-driven demand forecasting can significantly improve forecasting accuracy, leading to better decision-making, optimized operations, and a more competitive position in the market.

Practical Example: AI to Predict Product Demand and Optimize Inventory Levels

A company that sells consumer electronics online wants to optimize its inventory levels by predicting product demand. Using AI algorithms, they analyze historical sales data to forecast future demand for various products. The goal is to maintain optimal stock levels—ensuring that popular products don't run out of stock while preventing overstocking of slower-moving items. The company gathers historical sales data for the past 12 months and uses it to predict the expected sales for the next 3 months. With this information, they can adjust their inventory purchasing decisions, align production schedules, and optimize storage costs.

Sample Historical Sales Data (Units Sold)

Month	Product A	Product B	Product C	Product D	Product E
January	120	80	200	50	30
February	150	75	210	60	35
March	180	85	220	55	40
April	160	90	230	65	45
May	170	95	240	70	50
June	200	110	250	80	60
July	210	120	260	85	65

Month	Product A	Product B	Product C	Product D	Product E
August	220	130	270	90	70
September	180	100	250	75	55
October	190	110	260	80	60
November	200	120	280	85	65
December	230	140	300	95	70

AI Predicted Demand for Next 3 Months (January to March)

Month	Product A (Predicted)	Product B (Predicted)	Product C (Predicted)	Product D (Predicted)	Product E (Predicted)
January	225	130	310	100	75
February	235	135	320	110	80
March	240	140	330	115	85

Output and Results

1. **Product A**: The AI predicts a steady increase in demand over the next three months. From 200 units in December to 240 units in March, indicating growing popularity.

2. **Product B**: Product B's demand is also predicted to rise slowly, starting at 130 units in January, climbing to 140 in March.

3. **Product C**: This product has a substantial demand increase, with predicted sales reaching 330 units by March, suggesting it is in high demand.

4. **Product D**: A modest but consistent increase in demand for Product D is expected, growing from 95 in December to 115 by March.

5. **Product E**: Predicted demand shows a steady increase from 70 units in December to 85 units in March.

Observations and Decisions from an E-Commerce Perspective

- **Stocking Adjustments**: The company should order higher stock levels for Products A, C, and D as these show strong and consistent demand growth.

- **Prioritize Storage**: Products with high demand increases, like Product C, will require more warehouse space.

- **Supply Chain Coordination**: The predicted demand growth for Products A, B, and C may require adjustments in supply chain planning, ensuring timely replenishment to meet customer needs.

- **Marketing and Promotions**: Products like Product C and Product D may benefit from targeted promotions in the upcoming months to capitalize on the increased demand.

- **Overstock Risk**: Product E, though showing growth, is less critical and may not need significant stock increases unless future trends suggest a sharper rise in demand.

Conclusion

The AI-driven prediction allows the e-commerce company to take proactive steps to avoid stockouts or overstock situations, which is crucial for maintaining customer satisfaction and controlling operational costs. By aligning inventory levels with predicted demand, the company can ensure smoother operations and a more efficient supply chain.

6.2 Automating Supply Chain Decisions Using AI

Automating supply chain decisions using AI involves using advanced technologies to streamline operations, reduce human error, and improve overall efficiency. AI can process vast amounts of data much faster than humans, enabling real-time decision-making. With the integration of AI, supply chains become more responsive, as AI can predict demand, optimize inventory levels, and adjust procurement strategies based on evolving patterns in the market. This reduces the chances of overstocking or stockouts, ensuring products are available when needed without unnecessary costs.

Machine learning algorithms, a core component of AI, play a significant role in automating supply chain decisions. These algorithms can analyze historical data, market trends, and other factors to predict future demand accurately. By forecasting what products will be in demand and when, businesses can plan production and inventory more effectively. The result is a smoother supply chain that can adapt quickly to changes, whether due to seasonal variations or unexpected disruptions.

AI is also helpful in managing logistics, particularly in optimizing delivery routes. Traditional methods of route planning are often slow and rigid, but AI can continuously assess traffic patterns, weather conditions, and other variables to choose the most efficient delivery routes in real time. This not only saves time and costs but also enhances customer satisfaction by ensuring that products are delivered on time, every time. Furthermore, AI can predict maintenance needs for vehicles and equipment, preventing breakdowns and delays before they occur.

Another advantage of AI in supply chain automation is the ability to enhance supplier management. AI can analyze supplier performance based on factors like delivery times, quality, and costs. By automating supplier selection and negotiation processes, businesses can quickly identify the best partners and manage relationships more effectively. This also helps in risk management, as AI can assess the stability of suppliers and alert businesses about potential disruptions before they happen.

AI-powered systems can also improve inventory management. Instead of relying on manual stock tracking and replenishment, AI can automate these processes, ensuring that the right amount of inventory is always available. By continuously monitoring inventory levels, AI can predict when to reorder products, which helps prevent both understocking and overstocking. Additionally, AI can optimize warehouse layouts and manage the flow of goods more efficiently, reducing the time and effort required for inventory handling.

Overall, automating supply chain decisions using AI provides companies with more agility, efficiency, and accuracy in their operations. By reducing reliance on manual processes and enhancing decision-making, AI enables businesses to focus on innovation and customer satisfaction. The ongoing evolution of AI technologies will continue to refine these processes, making supply chains even more intelligent and capable of adapting to changing market conditions.

Practical Example: Optimizing Delivery Routes and Schedules with AI for E-Commerce Logistics

An e-commerce company that ships products to customers across multiple cities wants to improve its delivery efficiency by optimizing routes and schedules. The company uses AI algorithms such as machine learning models and genetic algorithms to analyze historical shipping data and optimize supply chain operations, reducing delivery times and costs. The sample data includes information about orders, shipping costs, delivery times, and locations.

Sample Data (Before Optimization)

Order ID	Customer Location	Shipping Distance (km)	Delivery Time (hrs)	Shipping Cost ($)
1	City A	100	5	50
2	City B	150	7	70
3	City C	200	9	90
4	City A	120	6	60
5	City D	180	8	80
6	City B	130	6.5	65
7	City D	160	7.5	75
8	City C	210	10	95

Optimization Process

Using AI, the company implements an optimization model that minimizes the total shipping cost and delivery time by adjusting the delivery routes and schedules. AI algorithms analyze factors such as traffic patterns, weather, and historical delays to generate optimized delivery routes.

Optimized Delivery Routes and Schedules

Order ID	Customer Location	Optimized Shipping Distance (km)	Optimized Delivery Time (hrs)	Optimized Shipping Cost ($)
1	City A	95	4.5	45
2	City B	145	6.5	65
3	City C	190	8	85
4	City A	110	5.5	55
5	City D	170	7	75
6	City B	120	6	60
7	City D	150	7	70
8	City C	200	9	90

Output and Results Interpretation:

1. **Shipping Distance and Delivery Time**: The optimized routes have reduced the shipping distances for most orders, especially for City A, where the distances decreased from 100 km to 95 km for Order 1, and from 120 km to 110 km for Order 4. Delivery times have also been shortened by an average of 30 minutes per order.

2. **Shipping Cost**: The optimized delivery routes have reduced the shipping costs. For example, Order 1 saw a cost reduction from $50 to $45, and Order 2 from $70 to $65.

Observations:

1. **Efficiency Gains**: The AI optimization has resulted in a reduction in both delivery times and shipping costs across all orders, suggesting significant improvements in logistics efficiency.

2. **Geographical Considerations**: Routes that cover shorter distances between cities lead to a noticeable reduction in costs. The optimization also considers potential delays from city congestion, allowing for smoother transitions and fewer stops.

3. **Cost-effectiveness**: In terms of cost savings, each optimized delivery route has resulted in an average reduction of about 5-10% in shipping costs.

Decisions from the E-Commerce Perspective:

1. **Reduced Shipping Costs**: By adopting AI-driven optimization, the company can reduce logistics costs, which directly impacts profitability. They can either offer lower shipping costs to customers or retain the savings to improve overall margins.

2. **Faster Deliveries**: With shorter delivery times, customers are likely to experience faster shipping, improving customer satisfaction and potentially increasing repeat business.

3. **Scalability**: The AI system can scale to accommodate growing orders and adapt to changing conditions (e.g., new cities or high-demand periods), providing long-term value as the company expands its operations.

In conclusion, AI-powered logistics optimization results in both tangible cost savings and improved service levels, aligning with key e-commerce objectives of cost efficiency, speed, and customer satisfaction.

6.3 AI for Inventory Replenishment and Stock Optimization

Inventory replenishment and stock optimization are crucial components of supply chain management, aiming to ensure that products are available when needed while minimizing excess stock. Using AI in this process helps businesses achieve a delicate balance between supply and demand, reducing the risks of both stockouts and overstocking. Traditional methods of inventory management are often time-consuming and error-prone, but AI can automate and optimize decisions, leading to more efficient stock control.

AI-based systems analyze vast amounts of historical data, including sales trends, seasonal demand fluctuations, and external factors such as market conditions or promotions. These insights allow AI algorithms to predict future demand more accurately, enabling businesses to replenish their stocks at the right time and in the right quantities. This predictive ability is crucial for reducing excess inventory, which can incur storage costs and tie up capital, while also preventing stockouts that may lead to lost sales and customer dissatisfaction.

One key advantage of AI in inventory management is its ability to learn and adapt over time. Machine learning models continuously improve their predictions based on new data, enabling businesses to respond to changing market conditions quickly. For example, if a particular product experiences a sudden surge in demand, AI systems can adjust inventory levels in real time to meet this increase. This adaptability ensures that businesses are always prepared for shifts in consumer behavior or unexpected disruptions in supply chains.

AI can also optimize inventory across multiple locations, helping companies manage stock levels in warehouses, retail outlets, and distribution centers. By coordinating replenishment efforts across various points in the supply chain, AI ensures that resources are allocated efficiently. For example, products that are overstocked in one location can be transferred to another where demand is higher, reducing the need for additional orders and minimizing the risks of inventory shortages.

Automation plays a significant role in improving stock management with AI. Through AI-driven systems, many manual processes, such as order generation and stock auditing, can be automated. This not only saves time but also reduces the chances of human errors that could lead to inventory discrepancies. Automation allows businesses to focus on more strategic tasks, such as planning for growth or optimizing product assortments, while AI handles the operational aspects of inventory management.

Incorporating AI into inventory replenishment strategies can result in cost savings, increased operational efficiency, and better customer satisfaction. By providing real-time insights and recommendations, AI systems empower businesses to make data-driven decisions that lead to optimized stock levels. This integration of AI into inventory and stock management ultimately helps companies achieve greater profitability and customer loyalty while maintaining a smooth and responsive supply chain.

Practical Example: Automating Inventory Replenishment Using AI Based on Real-Time Sales Data

In an e-commerce business, managing stock levels efficiently is crucial to prevent both stockouts and overstocking. By integrating AI with the sales and inventory data, the system can predict future demand, automatically reorder items, and optimize stock levels. For example, consider a small online store that sells electronics. The AI system can track sales patterns and trigger reorders when inventory falls below a predefined threshold, ensuring stock availability without manual intervention.

Sample Sales and Inventory Data

Product ID	Product Name	Current Stock	Daily Sales Average	Reorder Threshold	Lead Time (Days)	Predicted Sales in Lead Time	Reorder Quantity	Reorder Triggered
001	Bluetooth Headset	50	20	30	7	140	90	Yes
002	Wireless Mouse	80	15	40	5	75	40	No
003	Smart Watch	10	30	20	10	300	310	Yes

Product ID	Product Name	Current Stock	Daily Sales Average	Reorder Threshold	Lead Time (Days)	Predicted Sales in Lead Time	Reorder Quantity	Reorder Triggered
004	Laptop Charger	120	5	25	3	15	0	No

Output and Results Interpretation:

1. **Product 001 (Bluetooth Headset):**
   - ○ Current stock: 50 units, average daily sales: 20 units.
   - ○ Predicted sales in the next 7 days: 140 units.
   - ○ Reorder threshold is set at 30, and the current stock is well below the threshold after predicting future sales.
   - ○ **Reorder Triggered**: Yes, an order for 90 units is recommended to maintain stock levels.

2. **Product 002 (Wireless Mouse):**
   - ○ Current stock: 80 units, average daily sales: 15 units.
   - ○ Predicted sales in the next 5 days: 75 units.
   - ○ The predicted sales (75 units) are less than the current stock (80 units), so no reorder is needed.
   - ○ **Reorder Triggered**: No.

3. **Product 003 (Smart Watch):**
   - ○ Current stock: 10 units, average daily sales: 30 units.
   - ○ Predicted sales in the next 10 days: 300 units.
   - ○ The stock is insufficient for the predicted demand, and the reorder threshold (20 units) is breached.
   - ○ **Reorder Triggered**: Yes, an order for 310 units is recommended.

4. **Product 004 (Laptop Charger):**
   - ○ Current stock: 120 units, average daily sales: 5 units.

- o Predicted sales in the next 3 days: 15 units.
- o The current stock is sufficient to cover the predicted demand.
- o **Reorder Triggered**: No.

Observations and Decisions from an E-Commerce Perspective:

1. **Replenishment Efficiency**: The AI system ensures timely restocking based on real-time data. For example, products like the Bluetooth headset and smart watch are automatically reordered before they run out, minimizing the risk of stockouts.

2. **Cost Management**: The system helps to avoid overstocking, which can tie up capital in unsold inventory. In this case, products like the wireless mouse and laptop charger don't require reordering, which prevents unnecessary purchasing.

3. **Inventory Optimization**: The AI system's predictions are designed to align with actual sales trends, enhancing inventory management. By accurately predicting demand and adjusting orders accordingly, the business can reduce excess stock while ensuring availability.

4. **Operational Automation**: Manual stock monitoring and ordering processes are replaced with automated AI-driven decisions, saving time and reducing human error in the supply chain.

In conclusion, leveraging AI to automate stock replenishment based on real-time sales data allows e-commerce businesses to optimize their inventory management, improve customer satisfaction by preventing stockouts, and enhance operational efficiency.

7. Visual Search and Image Recognition in E-Commerce

Visual search and image recognition technologies have become increasingly important in e-commerce. These technologies allow consumers to search for products using images instead of text. By uploading or taking pictures of items they are interested in, shoppers can quickly find similar or identical products available for purchase. This enhances the user experience by offering a more intuitive and efficient way to browse, especially when a specific item is hard to describe in words.

For retailers, integrating visual search and image recognition into their platforms can significantly improve conversion rates. Customers are more likely to find what they are looking for, reducing frustration and increasing the likelihood of completing a purchase. This can also streamline the buying process, as customers don't need to manually filter through categories or enter detailed search terms. The technology also allows for more personalized recommendations, as products can be suggested based on visual similarities to the items already browsed or purchased.

Image recognition technology works by analyzing various features within an image, such as shapes, colors, and textures, and matching those features with products in the retailer's inventory. Machine learning algorithms play a crucial role in improving the accuracy of these systems over time. The more data the system processes, the better it becomes at identifying products accurately and matching them with relevant items from the catalog. This continuous learning process enhances both the speed and precision of the search results.

This capability has the potential to transform online shopping, as it reduces the gap between physical and digital retail experiences. In traditional stores, customers can easily pick up and inspect products, but online shoppers rely on product descriptions and reviews. Visual search bridges this gap, providing a more tactile shopping experience by allowing users to visually compare products. This is particularly beneficial in fashion, home decor, and even food and beverage sectors, where aesthetic details are crucial to the purchasing decision.

Furthermore, visual search can enhance social commerce. Many users share images of products on social media, which can influence their followers' buying decisions. By using image recognition, retailers can allow users to search for similar items based on images they encounter on these platforms. This creates a seamless shopping experience between social media and e-commerce, leveraging the influence of user-generated content and social proof to drive sales.

Despite the many advantages, challenges remain. Image recognition systems need to be accurate enough to handle a wide variety of images and contexts. Variations in lighting, angles, and image quality can affect the system's performance. Additionally, privacy concerns surrounding the collection and use of user data for visual search purposes must be addressed. However, as the technology continues to improve, its potential to reshape the e-commerce landscape remains significant, providing a more dynamic and user-friendly shopping experience.

Practical Example Context:

In an e-commerce setting, a customer is browsing for shoes online but is unable to find the exact style they are looking for. Using visual search and image recognition, the customer uploads a photo of a shoe they like. The e-commerce platform then utilizes AI-based image recognition to analyze the uploaded photo and match it with products in its database. The platform returns results that display similar shoes with details about pricing, color options, and availability. This visual search capability enhances the user experience by simplifying product discovery.

Sample Data:

Product ID	Product Name	Price	Similarity Score	Availability	Product Category	Match Confidence (%)
1001	Classic Leather Shoe	$79.99	95%	In Stock	Shoes	98%
1002	Modern Sneakers	$59.99	92%	Out of Stock	Shoes	95%
1003	Casual Walking Shoe	$69.99	89%	In Stock	Shoes	90%
1004	Stylish Ankle Boots	$89.99	85%	In Stock	Shoes	85%
1005	Outdoor Hiking Boots	$99.99	80%	In Stock	Shoes	80%

Output and Results:

- The e-commerce platform uses image recognition to analyze the shoe in the uploaded photo, comparing features such as design, material, and structure.

- The **Similarity Score** reflects how closely the item in the database matches the uploaded image (higher score indicates a closer match).

- **Match Confidence (%)** indicates the AI system's certainty that the suggested product matches the photo.

Explanation and Interpretation of Results:

- The **Classic Leather Shoe** with a 95% similarity score and 98% match confidence appears to be the closest match to the shoe in the customer's photo, with high availability. This could be the most relevant recommendation to display.

- **Modern Sneakers** have a similarity score of 92%, but they are out of stock, which makes them less ideal for immediate purchase.

- Other items like the **Casual Walking Shoe** and **Stylish Ankle Boots** also show strong similarity (89% and 85%, respectively), but their match confidence and similarity scores are lower than the top choice.

- **Outdoor Hiking Boots** have the lowest similarity score and confidence, indicating a less relevant match to the original shoe.

Observations:

- The **Classic Leather Shoe** is the best match in terms of similarity score and availability, making it the optimal suggestion for the customer.

- The **Out of Stock** status for some products limits their usefulness, suggesting the need for better stock management or recommendation systems to account for product availability.

- The system seems to prioritize matching based on product features, but it also needs to consider factors like pricing, style preference, and availability more comprehensively.

Decisions from an E-Commerce Perspective:

1. **Promote Available Products**: The system should prioritize recommending items with high match confidence and stock availability (e.g., the Classic Leather Shoe).

2. **Enhance User Experience**: Incorporate filters for availability, price range, and color options in the visual search results to refine recommendations.

3. **Inventory Management**: Ensure that popular products are consistently in stock to minimize the chances of showing out-of-stock items.

4. **Further Optimization**: The visual recognition model could be trained to consider additional factors like customer reviews, ratings,

and specific customer preferences (e.g., eco-friendly materials or specific colors) for a more personalized experience.

By using visual search and image recognition technologies, the e-commerce platform improves product discovery, increases user engagement, and boosts the likelihood of successful transactions.

7.1 AI-Powered Visual Search for Product Discovery

AI-powered visual search has revolutionized the way people discover and interact with products online. By using machine learning algorithms and computer vision, visual search enables users to search for products through images rather than text-based queries. This technology recognizes objects within an image and matches them to similar products in a retailer's catalog, offering a seamless and efficient browsing experience. As a result, consumers no longer need to rely on keywords or descriptions, as visual search allows for more intuitive and precise discovery.

The core of visual search relies on sophisticated image recognition, which analyzes various elements such as color, shape, texture, and patterns. This technology has improved significantly over the years, enabling it to identify even highly detailed and complex items accurately. Users can simply upload a photo of an item they are interested in, and the AI system will provide results that closely match the item's features. This approach eliminates the limitations of traditional search methods, where users may struggle to describe products in the right way.

For businesses, integrating AI-powered visual search provides a competitive advantage. It allows retailers to offer more personalized shopping experiences, as the system can suggest similar products based on the visual characteristics of an item. Additionally, by using visual search, companies can improve their product recommendations and optimize their inventory management. With more customers turning to mobile devices for online shopping, visual search is especially effective in capturing attention and driving conversions.

The adoption of AI visual search has also led to the creation of new customer touchpoints. Social media platforms, for example, have integrated visual search features that allow users to discover products directly from images they come across in posts or ads. This adds a layer of convenience and encourages impulse buying, as users can easily identify and purchase products without leaving the platform. This integration of visual search in social media has expanded the ways in which consumers interact with brands.

One of the key benefits of visual search is its ability to reduce the friction in the discovery process. It addresses a common pain point for online shoppers: the difficulty in finding exactly what they want. Instead of typing out a long description or filtering through numerous categories, users can simply upload an image and receive an instant, accurate result. This simplicity not only saves time but also increases satisfaction, which can lead to higher customer loyalty and repeat business.

Despite its many advantages, there are still challenges to overcome in the widespread implementation of visual search. While the technology has made significant strides, it can still struggle with distinguishing certain objects or understanding context. Moreover, privacy concerns around data collection and the ethical use of AI remain prominent. However, as the technology continues to evolve and improve, AI-powered visual search holds the potential to reshape the e-commerce landscape and change the way consumers discover and purchase products online.

Practical Example of Implementing Visual Search in E-Commerce for Seamless Shopping Experiences

In an e-commerce platform, implementing visual search enables customers to upload an image and find similar products available for purchase. For example, if a customer uploads an image of a red leather jacket, the system uses computer vision algorithms to identify key features like color, texture, and shape. The visual search engine then matches the uploaded image with similar items in the platform's product database. The goal is to enhance the shopping experience by allowing users to find products quickly without needing to describe them in words.

Sample Data

Below is a table showing the results from a visual search query where a customer uploaded an image of a red leather jacket:

Image ID	Product Name	Image Match Confidence (%)	Product Category	Price ($)	Similarity Score (%)
101	Red Leather Jacket A	95	Jackets	120	98
102	Burgundy Leather Bomber	90	Jackets	110	92
103	Red Faux Leather Jacket B	85	Jackets	100	87

Image ID	Product Name	Image Match Confidence (%)	Product Category	Price ($)	Similarity Score (%)
104	Dark Red Leather Trench Coat	80	Jackets	150	85
105	Bright Red Leather Blazer	88	Blazers	130	91

Output and Results

1. **Confidence Score**: This column indicates how closely the visual search system believes the uploaded image matches the products listed in the database. Higher values suggest stronger matches.

2. **Similarity Score**: The percentage indicates how similar each product is to the uploaded image in terms of visual features such as color, shape, and texture.

3. **Product Relevance**: Products with higher confidence and similarity scores (like the Red Leather Jacket A with 98%) are more likely to be of interest to the customer.

Interpretation of Results

- **Red Leather Jacket A** has the highest match confidence (95%) and similarity score (98%), suggesting it is the most accurate recommendation based on the uploaded image. This would be the top recommendation for the customer.

- **Burgundy Leather Bomber** and **Red Faux Leather Jacket B** also have strong matches, with similarity scores of 92% and 87%, respectively, indicating that they are good alternatives, although not perfect matches.

- **Dark Red Leather Trench Coat** and **Bright Red Leather Blazer** are somewhat less relevant due to their lower similarity and confidence scores, but they might still appeal to the customer depending on their preference for slight variations in style or color.

Observations

- The system successfully identifies visually similar products, enhancing the user experience by offering intuitive search results.

- The closer the similarity score to 100%, the better the match, but a score above 85% can still offer valuable alternatives.

- Products in the same or related categories (e.g., jackets, blazers) are likely to be considered, even if they are not exact matches, providing the customer with a range of options.

Decisions from an E-Commerce Perspective

1. **Optimize for High-Confidence Matches**: Products with high match confidence should be displayed first to increase the likelihood of conversion, as they are the closest matches to the customer's request.

2. **Show Alternatives with Lower Similarity**: Present alternatives with slightly lower similarity scores as "related products" to keep customers engaged with a broader selection. These can be recommended as additional choices in case the top match does not meet the customer's preferences.

3. **Improve Visual Search Accuracy**: Continuously refine the visual search algorithm to improve the match confidence, reducing irrelevant product recommendations.

4. **Personalization**: Use customer data (e.g., purchase history, preferences) to tailor search results, making the visual search even more relevant to individual users.

7.2 Product Image Recognition for Cataloging and Tagging

Product image recognition is a powerful tool used for cataloging and tagging items in various industries, especially retail and e-commerce. By using advanced machine learning algorithms, it enables systems to automatically identify objects, classify them into categories, and assign relevant tags. This process eliminates the need for manual input, reducing human error and improving efficiency in managing large product inventories. The software can process product images and recognize key features such as shape, color, size, and texture, which are essential for proper categorization.

With the increasing amount of visual data in online shopping platforms, automation of product tagging has become crucial for both retailers and consumers. Accurate product categorization helps enhance searchability and improves the overall shopping experience. For example, when a customer searches for a particular type of item, such as "leather jacket," the recognition system ensures that all relevant products are displayed. Additionally, tagging products with relevant descriptors like "formal," "outdoor," or "winter" helps customers quickly find exactly what they are looking for, boosting sales and satisfaction.

The recognition technology also aids in organizing and updating inventory with minimal human intervention. When new products are added to a catalog, the system can automatically identify and categorize them based on the visual data provided. This ensures that the inventory remains up to date without requiring constant manual effort, which is especially beneficial in fast-moving industries like fashion or electronics. Furthermore, this system can be integrated with existing inventory management tools to keep track of stock levels, making it easier to predict demand and adjust procurement accordingly.

One of the challenges in implementing image recognition for cataloging is ensuring that the algorithms are accurate and can handle a wide variety of product types and image qualities. Variations in lighting, angles, and backgrounds can all affect the performance of the system. For instance, a poorly lit image of a product may lead to incorrect classification or tagging. However, as machine learning models continue to improve, they become better at distinguishing between objects in challenging conditions, making the technology more robust over time.

Moreover, the use of image recognition for product tagging also helps businesses in their marketing efforts. With detailed, accurate tagging, companies can target customers with personalized recommendations and advertisements based on the products they are most likely to be interested in. This data-driven approach allows businesses to increase engagement and drive conversions, making product image recognition not just a tool for inventory management but a critical component of customer engagement and sales strategies.

In conclusion, product image recognition plays a pivotal role in modernizing the cataloging and tagging process across various industries. By automating categorization, improving inventory management, and enabling personalized customer experiences, this technology helps businesses stay competitive in a fast-paced market. As machine learning and computer vision continue to evolve, the capabilities of product image recognition will only grow, offering even more sophisticated solutions to streamline operations and enhance user experience.

Practical Example: Using AI to Automatically Tag and Categorize Product Images on an E-Commerce Platform

Imagine an e-commerce platform that sells a wide variety of products like clothing, electronics, home goods, and accessories. In this scenario, an AI-based image recognition system is deployed to automatically tag and categorize product images based on their content. This saves the manual effort of tagging each product image and enhances the platform's searchability and user experience. The AI system is trained on vast datasets of labeled images and uses techniques like deep learning to classify and generate relevant tags for each product image.

Sample Data of Product Images and AI-Generated Tags:

Product Image ID	Product Name	AI-Generated Tags	Predicted Category	Confidence Score
101	Smart Watch	smartwatch, wearable, tech, fitness, gadget	Electronics	98%
102	Running Shoes	shoes, athletic, sports, running, footwear	Apparel & Footwear	95%

Product Image ID	Product Name	AI-Generated Tags	Predicted Category	Confidence Score
103	Leather Jacket	jacket, leather, outerwear, fashion, winter	Apparel	92%
104	Wireless Headphones	headphones, wireless, audio, music, tech	Electronics	99%
105	Coffee Maker	coffee, kitchen, appliance, coffee maker, home	Home & Kitchen	96%

Output and Results:

- **Accuracy and Efficiency**: The AI system is able to tag the products with a high level of confidence, as indicated by the confidence scores (above 90% for all products).

- **Categorization**: The AI categorizes the products into relevant categories (e.g., Electronics, Apparel, Home & Kitchen), enabling customers to easily browse through the catalog.

- **Tagging**: Each product has relevant and precise tags (e.g., "tech," "gadget," "sports"), which make the search and filtering system more accurate.

Observations:

1. **Tagging Relevance**: The AI system does a good job of tagging products based on their characteristics. For example, the "Smart Watch" image is tagged with appropriate terms such as "wearable," "fitness," and "gadget," which makes sense for the target audience.

2. **Confidence Scores**: The confidence scores are consistently high (above 90%), which indicates that the model is likely well-trained and accurate in its predictions.

3. **Category Accuracy**: The AI assigns correct categories (e.g., "Wireless Headphones" under Electronics), ensuring that products appear in the correct sections on the platform.

Decisions from the E-Commerce Perspective:

1. **Improved Search and Discovery**: With accurate tags and categories, customers can easily find products by searching keywords or filtering by category, enhancing their shopping experience and potentially increasing sales.

2. **Reduced Manual Effort**: The automatic tagging and categorization process reduces the time and resources required for manual tagging, allowing the platform to scale more efficiently.

3. **Optimized Inventory Display**: Accurate categorization ensures that products are displayed in the right sections, leading to better organization and a more intuitive shopping experience.

4. **Personalized Recommendations**: With the detailed tags, AI can better suggest products based on user behavior and preferences, potentially boosting conversion rates.

5. **Ongoing AI Model Improvement**: The high confidence levels show that the AI model is performing well, but monitoring for misclassifications is important to continuously improve the model. For instance, further data or edge cases could be used to retrain the model for even more accurate results.

In summary, AI-driven image tagging and categorization can significantly enhance both the user experience and operational efficiency on an e-commerce platform.

7.3 Enhancing Product Listings with AI-Driven Image Optimization

AI-driven image optimization is transforming the way product listings are presented online, enabling businesses to improve visual appeal and customer engagement. With the increasing importance of e-commerce platforms, high-quality, attractive images can make a significant difference in capturing consumer attention. Traditional methods of image editing and enhancement often require manual intervention, but AI-powered tools can now automate this process, improving images in ways that are both efficient and effective.

One of the key advantages of AI-driven optimization is its ability to adjust image quality based on specific needs, such as enhancing brightness, contrast, and sharpness to make products appear more appealing. AI can also correct common flaws like blurry backgrounds or low resolution, creating a more professional and polished look without requiring human expertise. This automation allows businesses to produce large quantities of product images with minimal effort, which is especially beneficial for brands with extensive inventories.

In addition to improving image quality, AI tools can help resize and compress images to meet various platform requirements without compromising visual integrity. Different e-commerce platforms have different specifications for image size and format, and AI can adapt images to meet these criteria seamlessly. This process not only ensures that images load faster, improving website performance, but also saves businesses time and resources that would otherwise be spent manually adjusting each image.

AI can also enhance product images by detecting and removing background noise, ensuring the focus remains on the product itself. For example, AI tools can automatically replace cluttered or unappealing backgrounds with clean, neutral ones, which helps maintain the focus on the product's features and makes it easier for consumers to assess the item. This also leads to more visually consistent listings across different products, which can positively impact the brand's overall aesthetic and consumer trust.

Furthermore, AI-driven optimization can help improve accessibility. AI tools can automatically generate alternative text for images, describing the product and its features for those with visual impairments. By incorporating machine learning, these tools ensure that the descriptions are both accurate and relevant, providing a better experience for all users. This helps businesses align with accessibility guidelines and create a more inclusive shopping environment.

Lastly, AI optimization tools are constantly evolving, with new features and capabilities emerging to meet the changing demands of e-commerce. From enhancing image quality to ensuring faster load times and improving user experience, AI is proving to be a vital asset for online retailers looking to stay competitive in a crowded market. By leveraging AI-driven image optimization, businesses can not only improve their product listings but also drive higher conversion rates and customer satisfaction, ultimately boosting their sales and reputation.

Practical Example: Optimizing Product Images Using AI to Improve Visual Appeal and Conversion Rates

An e-commerce store selling high-end consumer electronics has decided to optimize its product images to enhance visual appeal and improve conversion rates. The product images were initially taken using a standard camera without professional lighting or post-processing. Using an AI-based image enhancement tool, the store improved the images by adjusting colors, enhancing lighting, and sharpening details to make the product more visually appealing. This optimization aims to see if improved image quality leads to higher conversion rates.

Sample Product Data:

Product ID	Original Image (Before AI)	Enhanced Image (After AI)	Click-Through Rate (CTR)	Conversion Rate (CR)	Bounce Rate (BR)	Time on Page (Minutes)
101			3.5%	2.1%	40%	3.2
102			4.0%	2.6%	35%	4.0
103			2.8%	1.8%	45%	2.5
104			5.2%	3.5%	30%	4.5
105			3.0%	2.0%	38%	3.0

Results and Output Interpretation:

Observations:

1. **Click-Through Rate (CTR):** After applying AI image enhancement, all products saw a notable increase in CTR. For example, Product ID 101 saw an increase from 3.5% to 4.0%, a jump of 0.5 percentage points. The highest increase was seen in Product ID 104, which had an increase of 0.8 percentage points (from 5.2% to 5.2%).

2. **Conversion Rate (CR):** The conversion rate also improved significantly for most products. Product 104 saw the most improvement in terms of conversion, going from 3.5% to 4.5%. AI-enhanced images likely led to better engagement and a stronger buying intent.

3. **Bounce Rate (BR):** The bounce rate decreased slightly across the board, indicating that users were spending more time engaging with the product pages after the image optimization. For example, Product ID 101 experienced a decrease from 40% to 35%.

4. **Time on Page:** AI-enhanced images also resulted in increased engagement, with visitors spending more time on product pages. For example, Product ID 104 increased its average time on page from 3.0 minutes to 4.5 minutes, which correlates with better engagement.

Decision-Making from an E-Commerce Perspective:

1. **Invest in AI-based Image Enhancement Tools:** The data clearly shows that improving product image quality through AI has a positive impact on both click-through rates and conversion rates. E-commerce businesses should consider using AI tools for image enhancement, particularly in visually intensive product categories like electronics, fashion, and luxury goods.

2. **Focus on High-Impact Products:** Products that had the largest improvements in performance (e.g., Product ID 104) should be prioritized for further optimization, as they offer the best return on investment in terms of increased conversions.

3. **Experiment with Further Image Optimization:** Since the results show improved metrics, experimenting with other aspects of image optimization (e.g., image backgrounds, zooming capabilities, or lifestyle imagery) could yield even better results. E-commerce sites

should test and iterate on different enhancements to maximize conversions.

4. **Monitor and Scale Up:** Based on the improvements observed, scaling the use of AI image enhancement across the entire product catalog could further boost performance, especially for products with lower CTR and conversion rates.

8. Fraud Detection and Prevention in E-Commerce

Fraud detection and prevention in e-commerce is a critical aspect of maintaining trust and safety in online transactions. As the number of online shoppers grows, so does the number of fraudulent activities.

E-commerce platforms are often targeted by cybercriminals who try to exploit weaknesses in payment systems, personal data security, and user authentication processes. Without effective fraud detection and prevention systems, businesses can face significant financial losses, damage to their reputation, and a decrease in customer loyalty.

One of the most common forms of fraud in e-commerce is payment fraud, where criminals use stolen credit card information or fake identities to make unauthorized purchases. To combat this, online merchants use various methods to verify the authenticity of transactions. These may include multi-factor authentication, real-time monitoring, and the use of encryption technologies to protect sensitive payment details. By implementing such measures, merchants can reduce the chances of fraudulent transactions being processed.

Another significant issue is account takeover, where fraudsters gain unauthorized access to customer accounts and make purchases or steal personal information. This type of fraud is often carried out using stolen login credentials, which can be obtained through phishing attacks or data breaches. To prevent account takeovers, businesses can implement stronger password policies, biometric verification, and anomaly detection systems that flag unusual account activity. These measures help ensure that only legitimate users can access their accounts.

In addition to transaction monitoring, businesses also rely on machine learning and artificial intelligence to detect patterns of fraud. These technologies analyze vast amounts of transaction data and can identify suspicious behavior that may go unnoticed by humans. For example, if a customer suddenly makes a large purchase from an overseas location, or if multiple transactions are made within a short period, AI algorithms can flag these actions for further investigation. This proactive approach helps e-commerce platforms stay one step ahead of fraudsters.

Customer education plays a vital role in fraud prevention as well. Many e-commerce fraud cases occur due to human error, such as customers unknowingly sharing their personal information with scammers. By educating customers about common types of fraud, such as phishing emails or fake websites, businesses can help them recognize and avoid potential threats. Providing clear guidelines on how to protect personal information and encouraging strong password practices can reduce the likelihood of fraud happening.

Finally, it is important to have a robust system in place for responding to fraud incidents when they do occur. This includes offering quick and efficient customer support, as well as a clear process for handling disputed transactions. E-commerce platforms should also cooperate with financial institutions and law enforcement agencies to investigate fraud and recover lost funds. By being transparent and proactive in handling fraud cases, businesses can maintain customer trust and mitigate the long-term impact of fraudulent activities.

Fraud Detection and Prevention in E-Commerce

In an e-commerce platform, fraud detection is essential to prevent financial losses from fraudulent activities such as credit card fraud, account takeovers, and fake returns. A typical approach to fraud detection involves using machine learning algorithms that analyze transaction data to detect patterns indicative of fraud. For example, a company might collect data on transaction attributes such as payment method, order value, shipping address, and account age to classify transactions as either legitimate or fraudulent.

Sample Data

Transaction ID	Customer ID	Order Value ($)	Payment Method	Account Age (Days)	Shipping Address Match	Previous Fraudulent Activity	Status
T001	C001	150.00	Credit Card	45	Yes	No	Legit
T002	C002	200.00	PayPal	120	No	Yes	Fraud
T003	C003	25.00	Credit Card	10	Yes	No	Legit
T004	C004	300.00	Credit Card	300	Yes	Yes	Fraud
T005	C005	50.00	Debit Card	80	No	No	Legit

Output & Results

Based on a fraud detection model, the algorithm flags T002 and T004 as fraudulent. Here's the breakdown of how each feature influences the decision:

1. **Transaction ID T001 (Legit)**: Despite a moderately high order value, this transaction is flagged as legitimate because the shipping address matches and there is no previous fraudulent activity.

2. **Transaction ID T002 (Fraud)**: This order is flagged as fraudulent because the account is relatively new (120 days), the shipping address does not match the registered one, and there is a history of previous fraudulent activity.

3. **Transaction ID T003 (Legit)**: Despite being a low-value transaction, the shipping address matches, and there is no record of previous fraud, so it is classified as legitimate.

4. **Transaction ID T004 (Fraud)**: This order has a high value, a history of previous fraud, and although the shipping address matches, the risk of a repeat fraudulent account triggers a fraud alert.

5. **Transaction ID T005 (Legit)**: Although the shipping address doesn't match, the lower order value and lack of fraudulent history on the account result in a legitimate classification.

Observations

- **Account Age and Fraud Risk**: Newer accounts (T002) are more likely to be flagged as fraudulent due to higher chances of being compromised or used for scams.

- **Shipping Address Mismatch**: Discrepancies between the shipping address and account address, as seen in T002 and T005, significantly increase the likelihood of fraud.

- **History of Fraudulent Activity**: Accounts with prior fraud incidents (T002 and T004) are often flagged for future transactions.

- **Transaction Value**: Higher value orders (T004) are often scrutinized more closely, as larger sums are more attractive for fraudsters.

E-Commerce Perspective Decisions

1. **For Transaction ID T002**: The company should investigate this order further. Given the red flags of a new account, shipping address mismatch, and previous fraud history, it may be appropriate to request additional verification or even cancel the order.

2. **For Transaction ID T004**: This transaction has multiple risk factors (high order value and previous fraud history), so it would be wise to flag this for manual review and potentially block the transaction.

3. **For Transaction IDs T001, T003, and T005**: These transactions seem safe based on current risk indicators, and no immediate action is required, but they should still be monitored for any changes in behavior or risk patterns in the future.

In summary, by using a machine learning model and analyzing data from multiple features, an e-commerce business can automate the identification of high-risk transactions and take preventive actions such as blocking or flagging suspicious orders for further investigation.

8.1 AI-Based Fraud Detection Systems

AI-based fraud detection systems are designed to help organizations identify and prevent fraudulent activities by leveraging machine learning, data analysis, and automation. These systems process large volumes of data, such as transaction histories, user behavior, and even network activity, to detect patterns and anomalies that may indicate fraudulent actions. By analyzing vast amounts of data in real-time, AI can quickly spot unusual behavior that human analysts might miss, offering a faster and more efficient approach to fraud detection.

One of the key features of AI-based fraud detection is its ability to learn and adapt over time. As the system is exposed to more data, it continually refines its models to improve accuracy. This learning process allows the system to recognize both known fraud patterns and emerging tactics used by criminals. For instance, AI can detect new forms of fraud even before they are widespread by identifying subtle shifts in behavior that deviate from the norm.

The use of AI also reduces the reliance on human intervention, which can be time-consuming and prone to error. Traditional fraud detection methods often involve manual reviews, which can lead to delays or mistakes, especially when handling large-scale data. AI systems, on the other hand, are able to operate continuously and without fatigue, ensuring that fraudulent transactions are flagged in real-time, which enhances the security and efficiency of financial operations.

Another benefit of AI-based fraud detection systems is their ability to minimize false positives. In traditional fraud detection systems, legitimate transactions can sometimes be flagged as fraudulent, leading to customer frustration and lost revenue. AI systems, however, are more precise in identifying fraud because they analyze a wide range of variables and learn from past mistakes. By considering multiple factors simultaneously, AI reduces the chances of incorrectly marking a valid transaction as suspicious.

Furthermore, AI-based fraud detection is particularly useful in industries where fraud tactics are constantly evolving, such as banking, insurance, and e-commerce. In these sectors, criminals often adapt their strategies to circumvent traditional security measures. With AI, fraud detection systems are continuously updated with new data, ensuring they stay ahead of evolving threats. The system's ability to adjust to new conditions means it can maintain a high level of effectiveness even as fraud tactics change.

In conclusion, AI-based fraud detection systems are transforming the way organizations combat fraud. By providing faster, more accurate, and adaptive fraud detection, these systems help to protect both businesses and consumers from financial losses. The ability to process and analyze large amounts of data in real-time, coupled with the capacity to learn from experience, makes AI an invaluable tool in the ongoing battle against fraud. As technology continues to evolve, AI-based solutions will likely play an even greater role in safeguarding against fraudulent activities.

Practical Example: Detecting Fraudulent Transactions on E-Commerce Platforms Using Machine Learning Algorithms

In an e-commerce setting, detecting fraudulent transactions is crucial for maintaining trust and ensuring the safety of financial transactions. Machine learning (ML) algorithms, such as Decision Trees, Random Forest, and Logistic Regression, can be employed to analyze past transactions and identify suspicious patterns that could indicate fraud. For this example, we use a sample set of transaction data containing the following features:

- **Transaction ID**: Unique identifier for each transaction.

- **Transaction Amount**: The total value of the transaction.

- **Customer Age**: The age of the customer making the purchase.

- **Transaction Time**: The timestamp when the transaction occurred.

- **Location**: Geographical location from where the transaction was initiated.

- **Device**: Type of device used for the transaction (e.g., mobile, desktop).

- **Fraud Label**: Target variable indicating whether the transaction was fraudulent (1) or not (0).

Here's a sample dataset:

Transaction ID	Amount ($)	Customer Age	Transaction Time	Location	Device	Fraud Label
1001	150.50	29	2025-01-10 12:30	New York	Mobile	0

Transaction ID	Amount ($)	Customer Age	Transaction Time	Location	Device	Fraud Label
1002	450.00	45	2025-01-10 14:15	California	Desktop	0
1003	1200.00	36	2025-01-10 16:00	Texas	Mobile	1
1004	30.75	21	2025-01-10 17:10	New York	Mobile	0
1005	890.00	50	2025-01-10 19:05	Florida	Desktop	1
1006	23.50	23	2025-01-10 20:15	Texas	Mobile	0

Applying a Machine Learning Algorithm (Logistic Regression):

Let's train a logistic regression model to predict whether a transaction is fraudulent or not. After training the model using historical transaction data (including both legitimate and fraudulent transactions), the algorithm will output predictions.

Sample Model Output (Predictions):

Transaction ID	Amount ($)	Customer Age	Transaction Time	Location	Device	Actual Fraud Label	Predicted Fraud Label
1001	150.50	29	2025-01-10 12:30	New York	Mobile	0	0
1002	450.00	45	2025-01-10 14:15	California	Desktop	0	0

Transaction ID	Amount ($)	Customer Age	Transaction Time	Location	Device	Actual Fraud Label	Predicted Fraud Label
1003	1200.00	36	2025-01-10 16:00	Texas	Mobile	1	1
1004	30.75	21	2025-01-10 17:10	New York	Mobile	0	0
1005	890.00	50	2025-01-10 19:05	Florida	Desktop	1	0
1006	23.50	23	2025-01-10 20:15	Texas	Mobile	0	0

Interpretation of Results:

- **Transaction ID 1001, 1002, 1004, 1006**: These transactions were correctly identified as non-fraudulent by the model (Predicted = Actual).

- **Transaction ID 1003**: The model correctly flagged the transaction as fraudulent (Predicted = Actual).

- **Transaction ID 1005**: The model falsely flagged this transaction as non-fraudulent, although it was actually fraudulent (False Negative).

Observations:

1. The machine learning model performed well on the majority of the transactions, accurately predicting the non-fraudulent transactions and identifying one fraudulent transaction (ID 1003).

2. There was a **false negative** in transaction ID 1005, where a fraudulent transaction was not detected.

3. The model's effectiveness depends on the quality and quantity of the training data, as well as the features it uses for prediction.

Decisions from the E-Commerce Perspective:

1. **Transaction Monitoring**: Transactions flagged as high-risk (e.g., transaction ID 1005) should be monitored manually by a fraud analyst for further verification, especially if the model might have missed them.

2. **Improvement of Model**: Since there was a false negative, the model can be improved by including more features such as customer behavior patterns, historical purchase data, or using ensemble methods (like Random Forest or Gradient Boosting) to reduce the chance of false negatives.

3. **Customer Experience**: Non-fraudulent transactions should continue to be processed smoothly, but any flagged transactions (even if they are false positives) may require a secondary verification step to prevent customer dissatisfaction.

Overall, machine learning can significantly enhance fraud detection, but constant monitoring and model refinement are essential to achieve the best results in identifying fraudulent activities.

8.2 AI for Payment Processing Security

In today's digital age, payment processing security is crucial to ensure safe transactions for both businesses and customers. As the volume of online transactions grows, so does the risk of fraud and cyberattacks. AI plays a significant role in improving security by detecting suspicious behavior and automating protective measures. Machine learning algorithms can analyze large datasets, identifying patterns that might indicate fraud, such as unusual transaction amounts, locations, or timings. This ability to monitor in real-time helps prevent fraudulent activity before it causes significant damage.

One of the key ways AI enhances security is through its ability to continuously learn and adapt. Traditional security systems might rely on fixed rules or thresholds to detect fraud, but these can be bypassed by new techniques. AI, on the other hand, can evolve as it is exposed to more data, refining its detection mechanisms to keep pace with emerging threats. This means AI-driven systems can better detect subtle, evolving fraud tactics that might otherwise go unnoticed.

In addition to detecting fraud, AI can help with identity verification. With the rise of digital wallets and online banking, confirming the identity of a person involved in a transaction is vital. AI can analyze biometric data such as facial recognition, fingerprints, or even behavioral patterns, enhancing the accuracy of identity verification. This reduces the chances of identity theft, where fraudsters impersonate legitimate users to conduct unauthorized transactions.

Another advantage of AI in payment processing security is its ability to reduce false positives. In traditional fraud detection systems, legitimate transactions can sometimes be flagged as fraudulent, leading to unnecessary delays or customer frustration. By using AI models that learn from both fraudulent and legitimate transaction data, the system becomes more precise in distinguishing between the two, ensuring a smoother customer experience while maintaining high security standards.

AI-powered systems also assist in compliance with regulations and industry standards. The payment industry is subject to various rules aimed at protecting consumer data, such as the General Data Protection Regulation (GDPR) or Payment Card Industry Data Security Standard (PCI DSS). AI can help ensure that companies meet these standards by automatically scanning for vulnerabilities or suspicious activities that may indicate a breach or non-compliance. This proactive approach saves businesses time and resources in maintaining regulatory compliance.

Finally, AI can improve the overall user experience by making payment systems more secure yet seamless. In addition to fraud prevention and identity verification, AI can optimize transaction processing by reducing the need for manual intervention or extensive customer authentication steps. This streamlining helps businesses operate more efficiently while offering consumers a faster, more secure way to conduct transactions. As AI continues to advance, it will remain an essential tool in maintaining the integrity and safety of payment processing systems.

Practical Example: Securing Payment Transactions Using AI to Identify Unusual Patterns and Anomalies

In an e-commerce platform, the goal is to identify potentially fraudulent transactions in real-time by analyzing payment data using AI-powered anomaly detection. The AI system can process historical transaction data, flagging transactions that deviate from typical behavior patterns (e.g., unusual amounts, locations, or frequency of payments). For instance, if a customer's account is suddenly used to make large purchases from a foreign country, this could trigger an alert for further investigation.

Sample Payment Transaction Data:

Transaction ID	Customer ID	Amount ($)	Location	Time of Transaction	Payment Method	Previous Transactions (last 30 days)	Fraudulent Activity Flag
1	12345	50	USA	2025-01-15 10:00 AM	Credit Card	5	No
2	12345	5000	USA	2025-01-15 11:30 AM	Credit Card	5	Yes
3	54321	100	UK	2025-01-14 02:00 PM	PayPal	3	No
4	12345	1000	Canada	2025-01-15 03:00 PM	Debit Card	5	Yes

Transaction ID	Customer ID	Amount ($)	Location	Time of Transaction	Payment Method	Previous Transactions (last 30 days)	Fraudulent Activity Flag
5	67890	200	USA	2025-01-13 08:00 PM	Credit Card	2	No
6	12345	3000	USA	2025-01-16 01:00 AM	Credit Card	5	Yes

AI-Powered Anomaly Detection:

The AI system analyzes the transactions, looking for patterns of unusual activity. It looks at parameters such as:

1. **Transaction Amount**: Large transactions compared to usual spending patterns.

2. **Geolocation**: Sudden purchases from unfamiliar or foreign locations.

3. **Time**: Unusual times for transactions (e.g., purchases late at night).

4. **Frequency**: A spike in the number of transactions within a short time frame.

Output and Results:

1. **Transaction ID 2**: A $5000 payment flagged as suspicious due to a large amount compared to previous transactions. Given the customer's average spending is under $200, this is a likely fraud risk.

2. **Transaction ID 4**: A $1000 payment from Canada, a location unfamiliar to the customer who has made all prior transactions in the USA, is flagged as suspicious.

3. **Transaction ID 6**: A $3000 purchase made in the middle of the night, unusual for this customer, triggers a fraud flag.

4. Other transactions with usual amounts, locations, and times (Transaction IDs 1, 3, 5) were not flagged as fraudulent.

Observations:

- **Frequent Transactions**: Customers with a history of numerous transactions within a short period may be at higher risk.

- **Location Changes**: A sudden change in geographical location can indicate a potential fraud attempt.

- **Amount Discrepancies**: Large payments outside of a customer's typical spending behavior (especially sudden large sums) are high risk.

Decisions from the E-Commerce Perspective:

1. **Transaction Verification**: Flagged transactions (ID 2, 4, 6) should undergo further manual verification. The system could request additional information, such as customer identity verification (e.g., through 2-factor authentication).

2. **Block Suspicious Transactions**: Transactions that show significant anomalies, especially from different locations or large amounts (e.g., ID 2, 4), could be automatically blocked pending investigation.

3. **Enhanced Monitoring**: For customers with flagged activities, increased monitoring could be implemented to detect further suspicious patterns.

4. **Machine Learning Model Tuning**: Continue to refine the AI model to better detect emerging fraud patterns based on new data.

The AI-powered anomaly detection significantly aids in reducing fraudulent activities and secures e-commerce transactions, enhancing customer trust while preventing losses.

8.3 Customer Behavior Analysis for Fraud Prevention

Customer behavior analysis plays a crucial role in fraud prevention by helping organizations understand and identify patterns of behavior that may signal suspicious or fraudulent activity. This analysis involves tracking various customer actions, such as purchase frequency, transaction amounts, geographic locations, and browsing habits, to establish a baseline of normal behavior. Once this baseline is established, any deviation from it can raise a red flag, indicating the possibility of fraud. For example, if a customer who typically makes small, local purchases suddenly initiates a large transaction from a foreign country, it could trigger an alert for further investigation.

The goal of customer behavior analysis is not just to detect fraud but also to differentiate between legitimate customer actions and potentially fraudulent ones. This distinction is vital to prevent false positives, where genuine customers are mistakenly flagged as fraudsters. By using advanced data analytics and machine learning models, organizations can accurately assess the likelihood of fraud and respond accordingly. These models continually learn from new data, making them increasingly effective at identifying emerging fraud trends and adapting to new tactics used by criminals.

A key component of behavior analysis is the use of historical data to predict future behavior. By studying past transactions and customer activity, businesses can identify early warning signs that might indicate an increased risk of fraud. For example, a sudden change in purchasing behavior, such as frequent, high-value transactions or unusual login patterns, could be an indicator that a fraudster has taken over an account. These insights allow organizations to implement proactive measures, such as temporarily freezing accounts or requiring additional authentication, before significant damage occurs.

Another important aspect of customer behavior analysis is monitoring for anomalous patterns that may indicate identity theft or account takeover. Fraudsters often gain access to legitimate customer accounts and use them for fraudulent purposes. Analyzing behavior such as multiple failed login attempts, changes to account details, or a sudden shift in location can provide insights into whether an account has been compromised. These behavioral changes can serve as an early warning system, helping businesses take swift action to secure the account and prevent further fraudulent activity.

Fraud prevention through behavior analysis also involves real-time monitoring. With the rise of e-commerce and digital transactions, it has become crucial for businesses to detect and respond to fraud in real time. Using automated systems that track customer behavior as transactions occur, businesses can flag suspicious activity instantaneously. This approach allows organizations to minimize the impact of fraud and protect both customers and their bottom line. Additionally, the real-time aspect of monitoring enables businesses to enhance the customer experience by reducing the chances of legitimate transactions being unnecessarily delayed or blocked.

Finally, the use of customer behavior analysis enhances the overall trust and security of a business. When customers are confident that their accounts and transactions are being monitored for fraud, they are more likely to engage with the business and make purchases. The combination of data analytics, machine learning, and real-time monitoring provides a robust framework for detecting and preventing fraud while maintaining a positive customer experience. This ultimately helps businesses safeguard their revenue, maintain customer loyalty, and protect their reputation in the market.

Practical Example

In an e-commerce environment, AI-based monitoring systems track user behavior patterns to detect suspicious activities, such as fraudulent purchases or account hacking. The system collects data on various user interactions, including login times, purchase frequency, abandoned carts, and sudden changes in browsing patterns. By analyzing this data, AI algorithms can flag activities that deviate from typical user behavior, indicating potential fraud or security issues.

Sample Data:

User ID	Login Frequency (per day)	Average Time Spent (mins)	Cart Abandonment Rate (%)	Purchase Frequency (per week)	Sudden Changes in Browsing (Yes/No)	Suspicious Activity Flag (Yes/No)
U001	3	15	20	2	No	No

User ID	Login Frequency (per day)	Average Time Spent (mins)	Cart Abandonment Rate (%)	Purchase Frequency (per week)	Sudden Changes in Browsing (Yes/No)	Suspicious Activity Flag (Yes/No)
U002	1	45	60	1	Yes	Yes
U003	5	10	10	5	No	No
U004	2	30	40	1	Yes	Yes
U005	10	5	80	10	Yes	Yes

Output and Results Interpretation

1. **User U001**: Regular behavior, low abandonment rate, and typical login frequency. No suspicious activity detected.

2. **User U002**: High cart abandonment rate and a sudden change in browsing behavior. Suspicious activity flagged due to abnormal patterns.

3. **User U003**: Frequent logins and regular purchases with low cart abandonment. No issues detected.

4. **User U004**: Moderate cart abandonment and a sudden change in browsing pattern. Suspicious activity flagged.

5. **User U005**: Excessive login frequency, high cart abandonment, and sudden change in browsing. Suspicious activity flagged due to irregular behavior.

Observations

- **User U002, U004, and U005** exhibit behaviors (such as high cart abandonment, sudden browsing changes, or excessive logins) that differ from typical user activity, triggering the suspicious activity flag.

- **User U001 and U003** maintain regular behavior patterns, indicating no suspicious activity.

Decisions from the E-Commerce Perspective

- **Investigate flagged users (U002, U004, U005)** for potential fraudulent activities. This could include verifying account security, cross-referencing purchase patterns with IP addresses, or reviewing payment methods.

- **Offer targeted interventions** like extra security checks for users exhibiting abnormal behavior.

- **Adjust fraud detection algorithms** to further refine the criteria for flagging suspicious activities based on observed patterns.

- **Customer Support Actions**: Proactively reach out to users with suspicious behavior to inquire about potential security concerns, offering password resets or account verification steps as needed.

9. Sentiment Analysis and Customer Feedback

Sentiment analysis is a technique used to understand the emotional tone behind a body of text, often applied to customer feedback to gauge how people feel about a product, service, or brand.

This method helps businesses comprehend not just the factual content but the emotions tied to that content, whether positive, negative, or neutral. It goes beyond just the words used; it takes into account context, intent, and even sarcasm to provide a clearer picture of customer sentiment. By analyzing large volumes of feedback, companies can extract meaningful insights about how their customers perceive their offerings.

Customer feedback plays a crucial role in shaping a company's strategy and improving its products or services. It acts as a direct line between the business and its customers, offering valuable insights into areas where the business excels and areas that need improvement. Collecting feedback through surveys, social media, or direct customer reviews is essential for businesses aiming to remain competitive in a dynamic market. It allows companies to track satisfaction levels and make data-driven decisions that address customer concerns, thereby enhancing customer loyalty.

The use of sentiment analysis in understanding customer feedback allows businesses to quickly assess large volumes of unstructured data. For instance, social media platforms and online reviews often generate massive amounts of feedback that can be overwhelming to process manually. Sentiment analysis tools can scan this data, categorize it, and highlight key trends in customer emotions. This automation saves time and resources, enabling businesses to act swiftly on customer concerns or capitalize on positive feedback that can be used for marketing or product development.

Businesses that consistently engage in sentiment analysis are better positioned to adapt to changing consumer preferences. If feedback reveals a negative sentiment toward a certain feature or aspect of the product, companies can take immediate steps to correct or modify it. On the other hand, positive sentiments can be amplified by promoting features that customers enjoy, further strengthening customer relationships. This responsiveness not only improves customer satisfaction but also builds trust and credibility with the audience.

A common challenge with sentiment analysis is that it might not always perfectly interpret the context of the language. For example, sarcastic comments or complex phrases may be misinterpreted by automated tools. Hence, it is important for companies to combine sentiment analysis with human oversight to ensure accuracy. Manual review may still be necessary to clarify ambiguous cases, particularly when dealing with highly specialized or emotional content. By striking a balance between automation and human judgment, companies can better understand their customers' true feelings.

The feedback gathered through sentiment analysis also serves as a foundation for long-term improvements. It can guide product development by highlighting customer pain points and desires, which can then be prioritized in future iterations. For example, if customers express frustration with a feature's usability, the business can focus on enhancing its design or functionality. Additionally, analyzing sentiment over time allows companies to measure the effectiveness of changes made in response to feedback, ensuring they continue to meet customer expectations and remain competitive in the marketplace.

Practical Example: Sentiment Analysis and Customer Feedback

In the context of e-commerce, sentiment analysis is often used to analyze customer feedback to gain insights into customer satisfaction, preferences, and potential areas for improvement. For instance, an online retail store could analyze reviews of a recently launched product to determine how customers feel about the product. Positive, negative, and neutral sentiments can be identified to help the store make better business decisions such as product improvements or marketing strategies.

Sample Data (Customer Feedback)

Customer ID	Review Text	Sentiment
1	"The product is great! It arrived on time and works as expected."	Positive
2	"Very disappointed. The product didn't work and was damaged."	Negative
3	"It's okay. Nothing special, but it works fine."	Neutral
4	"Excellent quality and fast shipping. Will definitely buy again."	Positive
5	"The packaging was bad, and the product didn't meet my expectations."	Negative
6	"Good value for money, and arrived on time."	Positive
7	"Not happy with the product, it broke within a week."	Negative
8	"Satisfied with the product. It works as described."	Positive
9	"The product is fine, but the customer service could be better."	Neutral
10	"Terrible experience. The item never arrived."	Negative

Output: Sentiment Distribution

Sentiment	Count	Percentage
Positive	4	40%
Negative	4	40%
Neutral	2	20%

Explanation and Interpretation

- **Sentiment Analysis Results:** Out of the 10 reviews analyzed, 40% of the feedback was positive, 40% was negative, and 20% was neutral.

- **Observations:**
  - Positive feedback indicates customer satisfaction with product quality, delivery, and overall experience. For example, reviews 1, 4, 6, and 8 are positive, showing that some customers were pleased with their purchases.
  - Negative feedback suggests issues such as product quality, delivery problems, or poor customer service. Reviews 2, 5, 7, and 10 express dissatisfaction, which could be a cause for concern.
  - Neutral feedback indicates that the customers were neither overly satisfied nor disappointed. Review 9 mentions dissatisfaction with customer service but does not criticize the product itself.

Decisions from an E-Commerce Perspective:

1. **Product Improvement:** The high amount of negative feedback suggests that the product has room for improvement. The store could consider looking into the quality issues mentioned in negative reviews and implement changes in design or functionality.

2. **Customer Service and Shipping:** Some reviews mention issues with shipping or packaging. The e-commerce store should assess and improve the logistics process to ensure timely and safe deliveries.

3. **Addressing Customer Service Issues:** Neutral reviews that mention poor customer service should prompt an internal review of

customer service protocols. Training and process improvements may be necessary to enhance customer satisfaction.

4. **Marketing Focus:** The positive reviews highlight the value and quality of the product. The store could leverage these aspects in marketing materials and promotions to attract more customers.

In summary, sentiment analysis provides actionable insights into customer feedback. The store can focus on improving product quality, enhancing shipping and customer service, and emphasizing positive aspects in its marketing campaigns to improve overall customer satisfaction and increase sales.

9.1 Analyzing Customer Reviews Using Sentiment Analysis

Sentiment analysis is a technique that helps to determine the emotional tone behind customer reviews. This process involves evaluating whether the reviews express positive, negative, or neutral sentiments, helping businesses understand customer experiences. By examining the language, words, and phrases used in the reviews, companies can gauge how customers feel about a product or service. This type of analysis provides insights into customer satisfaction and allows businesses to react promptly to improve or maintain their offerings.

Customer reviews often contain valuable information, but they can also be ambiguous or overly complex. Sentiment analysis tools use algorithms to break down these reviews, recognizing patterns that indicate positive or negative feelings. For instance, words like "excellent" or "love" suggest a positive sentiment, while words like "disappointing" or "poor" imply dissatisfaction. These tools can handle large volumes of reviews quickly, making it easier for businesses to monitor customer opinions consistently across various platforms.

One key advantage of sentiment analysis is that it enables businesses to track customer feedback on a large scale. With the increasing volume of online reviews, manually analyzing each one would be time-consuming and impractical. Automated sentiment analysis tools, however, can process thousands of reviews in a matter of seconds. This automation not only saves time but also helps businesses spot trends or emerging issues that might otherwise go unnoticed.

Moreover, sentiment analysis can highlight specific aspects of a product or service that customers either love or dislike. For example, customers might leave positive feedback about a product's quality but negative reviews about its packaging or delivery. By categorizing sentiment at a granular level, businesses can identify areas for improvement and prioritize changes that will have the most significant impact on customer satisfaction. This targeted approach is more efficient than attempting broad changes without understanding customer preferences.

In addition to helping businesses improve their products, sentiment analysis can be a powerful tool for competitive analysis. By examining the sentiment of reviews for competitors, companies can compare customer satisfaction levels and identify strengths or weaknesses in their own offerings. This can provide a competitive edge, as businesses can use insights from sentiment analysis to adjust their strategies or enhance their products based on customer feedback.

Ultimately, the insights gained from sentiment analysis are only valuable when acted upon. Businesses that regularly monitor and analyze customer sentiment can build stronger relationships with their audience. By responding to negative feedback in a timely manner or reinforcing positive experiences, companies can show that they value their customers' opinions. This proactive approach not only boosts customer loyalty but can also contribute to improved brand reputation and long-term success.

Practical Example Context:

In the context of an e-commerce platform, customer feedback is crucial for improving product offerings and services. By using sentiment analysis techniques, businesses can analyze customer reviews and assess their emotional tone (positive, neutral, or negative). For example, a company that sells home appliances may analyze customer reviews to determine whether the customers are satisfied with a particular product, what features they appreciate, and what areas need improvement. Sentiment analysis provides valuable insights that can guide product development, marketing strategies, and customer service improvements.

Sample Data (Product Reviews Analyzed Using Sentiment Analysis):

Review ID	Product	Customer Review	Sentiment
1	Smart Vacuum	"This vacuum works great! It picks up everything and is super easy to use."	Positive
2	Blender	"The blender is okay, but it makes a lot of noise and doesn't blend ice well."	Neutral
3	Coffee Maker	"I love this coffee maker! It brews fast, and the coffee tastes amazing."	Positive
4	Air Conditioner	"It stopped working after just a few days. Very disappointed."	Negative

Review ID	Product	Customer Review	Sentiment
5	Refrigerator	"The fridge is spacious, but the freezer section is not cold enough."	Neutral
6	Smart Vacuum	"Really bad purchase. The suction is weak, and it doesn't clean properly."	Negative
7	Blender	"Amazing blender, blends everything smoothly. Definitely recommend it!"	Positive
8	Coffee Maker	"The coffee maker is slow, and I had issues with the filter. Not happy."	Negative
9	Air Conditioner	"Works perfectly. Keeps my room cool even on the hottest days."	Positive
10	Refrigerator	"Great fridge, but the door seal doesn't close properly."	Neutral

Sentiment Analysis Output:

- **Positive Sentiment**: Reviews with positive language indicating satisfaction or delight (e.g., works great, love, amazing).
- **Neutral Sentiment**: Reviews with mixed feelings or average experiences (e.g., okay, spacious, but issues).
- **Negative Sentiment**: Reviews expressing dissatisfaction or frustration (e.g., stopped working, weak suction, not happy).

Interpretation of Results:

1. **Product Sentiment Distribution**:
   - **Smart Vacuum**: 1 positive, 1 negative (Balanced, potential for improvement).
   - **Blender**: 2 positive, 1 neutral (Generally positive feedback).
   - **Coffee Maker**: 1 positive, 1 negative (Mixed feelings, potential areas for improvement in speed and filter design).
   - **Air Conditioner**: 2 positive, 1 negative (Generally positive but occasional issues).

- o **Refrigerator**: 1 positive, 2 neutral (Functional, but some issues with specific features).

2. **Key Insights**:

- o **Smart Vacuum**: Customer feedback indicates a divide between satisfaction and dissatisfaction. The negative review points out poor suction, suggesting a need for better performance.

- o **Blender**: Positive feedback dominates. However, the neutral review about noise and ice blending might imply a need for improvements in noise reduction or blending efficiency for harder ingredients.

- o **Coffee Maker**: Mixed sentiments suggest issues with speed and filter functionality, indicating areas for product improvement.

- o **Air Conditioner**: Generally well-received, but occasional negative feedback highlights reliability issues.

- o **Refrigerator**: Neutral feedback with some concern over freezer performance and door seal. There's an opportunity to address these specific concerns.

Decisions from an E-Commerce Perspective:

1. **Product Development**:

- o Invest in improving vacuum suction power and overall performance based on customer dissatisfaction.

- o Focus on reducing noise and enhancing ice-blending functionality for the blender.

- o Consider redesigning the coffee maker's filter and improving its brewing speed.

- o For the air conditioner, ensure long-term durability and focus on troubleshooting reliability.

- o Improve freezer section cooling and the refrigerator's door seal to enhance customer satisfaction.

2. **Marketing and Customer Communication**:

- o Highlight positive aspects in product descriptions and marketing campaigns (e.g., fast brewing coffee makers, powerful air conditioners).

- o Address product weaknesses transparently in marketing materials to set proper expectations, such as noise levels for the blender.

- o Promote updates or versions of products that address common complaints (e.g., improved vacuum suction, better refrigerator seals).

3. **Customer Service**:

- o Respond proactively to negative feedback, especially when products like the vacuum or air conditioner experience failure.

- o Offer support for resolving specific issues (e.g., replacing defective vacuum models, offering troubleshooting tips for the coffee maker).

In conclusion, sentiment analysis provides actionable insights that can improve products, customer experience, and drive decisions based on real customer feedback.

9.2 Social Media Monitoring and Brand Sentiment

Social media monitoring refers to the process of tracking and analyzing online conversations and mentions across various platforms, such as Facebook, Twitter, Instagram, and blogs. Brands use this technique to gain insights into how their products, services, or industry are being discussed by the public. By employing social media monitoring tools, companies can track brand mentions, relevant keywords, hashtags, and customer feedback in real time. This helps brands stay aware of public perception and react promptly to both positive and negative interactions.

The main goal of social media monitoring is to gather data that provides an overview of what is being said about a brand. It helps identify key trends, track competitor activities, and evaluate the effectiveness of marketing campaigns. Monitoring allows businesses to understand how they are positioned in the market and which aspects of their brand are resonating with their audience. By actively listening to online conversations, businesses can also discover opportunities for improvement or innovation.

Brand sentiment analysis is closely related to social media monitoring and focuses on assessing the emotional tone behind online mentions. Sentiment analysis uses algorithms to categorize mentions as positive, neutral, or negative, helping brands gauge the overall public sentiment. This insight is crucial for understanding how consumers feel about a brand's products, services, or communications. A positive sentiment can indicate that a brand is well-received, while negative sentiment may reveal areas of concern or dissatisfaction that need addressing.

With the rise of social media, consumers have become more vocal about their experiences, making brand sentiment a critical component of reputation management. Negative sentiments, if not handled properly, can quickly escalate into a public relations crisis. Brands must act quickly to address issues raised in social media conversations, whether it's responding to customer complaints or correcting misinformation. On the other hand, positive sentiments offer an opportunity to build stronger relationships with customers by acknowledging their feedback and reinforcing brand loyalty.

In addition to monitoring general brand sentiment, businesses can use this information to improve their marketing strategies. For example, by analyzing the types of content that receive the most positive engagement, a brand can tailor future campaigns to align with customer preferences. Similarly, negative sentiments can be used to improve product offerings or customer service. Social media monitoring and sentiment analysis provide invaluable data for businesses looking to enhance their brand image and strengthen customer loyalty.

Overall, social media monitoring and brand sentiment analysis provide businesses with the tools to stay connected with their audience and react quickly to changes in public perception. As social media continues to play a central role in communication, understanding the mood of the online community is essential for businesses looking to maintain a positive public image. By combining real-time data with sentiment analysis, brands can stay ahead of potential issues and build a strong, trusted relationship with their customers.

Practical Example: Leveraging AI to Analyze Social Media Mentions and Assess Brand Sentiment

In an e-commerce context, a company wants to monitor its brand sentiment across social media platforms like Twitter, Facebook, and Instagram. Using AI tools, the company analyzes social media posts to assess customer sentiment toward its products and services. The AI tool processes mentions of the brand, categorizing them into positive, negative, or neutral sentiment. The company then aggregates these sentiments to understand how customers perceive the brand and to make informed decisions about marketing, customer service, and product development.

Sample Data from Social Media Mentions

Post ID	Platform	Mentions	Sentiment	Engagement Count
1	Twitter	"I love this new product!"	Positive	500
2	Facebook	"The quality could be better."	Negative	300
3	Instagram	"Great experience, highly recommend!"	Positive	700
4	Twitter	"Had an awful customer service experience."	Negative	200
5	Facebook	"Product is just okay."	Neutral	150
6	Instagram	"Fantastic service and fast delivery!"	Positive	800

Output and Results

Based on AI sentiment analysis, we can calculate the following sentiment distribution:

- **Positive Sentiment**: 4 posts (Twitter, Instagram, Facebook)
- **Negative Sentiment**: 2 posts (Twitter, Facebook)
- **Neutral Sentiment**: 1 post (Facebook)

The **Engagement Count** column shows the total engagement (likes, shares, comments) associated with each post. The company can weigh the sentiment based on engagement, giving more importance to posts with higher engagement.

Observations and Interpretation

- **Positive Sentiment**: Majority of mentions, particularly from Instagram and Twitter, express positive feedback with high engagement (e.g., Instagram post with 800 engagements). This is a strong indicator that customers are generally satisfied with the products and service.

- **Negative Sentiment**: While the negative mentions are fewer, they are still impactful due to lower engagement counts, indicating dissatisfaction, especially related to customer service. For example, the post about customer service on Twitter with 200 engagements highlights a potential area for improvement.

- **Neutral Sentiment**: The neutral mention indicates customers who are neither satisfied nor dissatisfied. While it doesn't provide a strong indication of customer sentiment, it can help highlight areas where the product might be improving or needs work.

Decisions from an E-Commerce Perspective

1. **Customer Service Improvement**: Given the negative sentiment about customer service, the company should prioritize improvements in this area to avoid customer churn and to ensure a positive brand perception. Additional training for customer service representatives could be a good action.

2. **Marketing Focus on Positive Sentiments**: The company should consider leveraging the positive mentions on Instagram and Twitter in marketing campaigns, as these posts have high engagement and can be used to build further brand loyalty.

3. **Product Development**: Neutral comments related to product quality should be analyzed in more detail to understand whether they reflect minor issues or potential areas for significant product improvement.

4. **Response Strategy**: For negative posts with lower engagement, the company should proactively reach out to the customers involved, offering solutions or apologies to mitigate any long-term damage to the brand's reputation.

In conclusion, AI-driven social media sentiment analysis offers valuable insights for e-commerce companies, enabling them to refine their strategies in customer service, marketing, and product development. By acting on these insights, businesses can improve customer satisfaction and brand perception.

9.3 Improving Customer Satisfaction with AI-Driven Insights

AI-driven insights are transforming the way businesses understand and respond to customer needs. By analyzing large volumes of data, AI can provide detailed insights into customer preferences, behaviors, and pain points. This enables businesses to personalize their offerings, ensuring that each interaction is tailored to the individual customer. As a result, companies can foster stronger relationships with their customers, enhancing satisfaction levels and encouraging brand loyalty.

The power of AI lies in its ability to process and analyze data faster and more accurately than humans. Through machine learning algorithms, AI systems can identify patterns and trends in customer feedback, social media interactions, and transaction histories. These insights help businesses anticipate customer needs, predict future behavior, and make informed decisions that directly impact customer satisfaction.

Another benefit of AI is its ability to deliver real-time recommendations and solutions. For example, AI-powered chatbots can provide immediate responses to customer queries, improving response times and reducing frustration. This on-demand service ensures that customers feel heard and valued, leading to more positive experiences. Moreover, AI can automate routine tasks, freeing up human agents to focus on more complex issues, further enhancing the customer support process.

AI tools also help companies identify areas where they may be falling short, allowing them to address issues before they escalate. Sentiment analysis, for instance, can track customer emotions expressed in online reviews or social media posts. If customers are consistently dissatisfied with a specific product or service, businesses can take corrective action quickly, showing customers that their concerns are being taken seriously and leading to better overall satisfaction.

Beyond individual interactions, AI can enhance customer satisfaction by optimizing the overall customer journey. By mapping out the customer's experience across various touchpoints, AI can highlight friction points that need improvement. Businesses can use these insights to streamline processes, reduce wait times, and simplify complex procedures, ensuring a smoother, more enjoyable experience for the customer.

Finally, AI-driven insights allow businesses to stay ahead of industry trends and customer expectations. With continuous learning and adaptation, AI systems can monitor emerging trends and consumer behavior shifts, providing businesses with the information they need to stay relevant. By aligning products, services, and marketing strategies with customer desires, companies can maintain high levels of satisfaction, ensuring long-term success in a competitive marketplace.

Practical Example: Using AI to Identify Customer Pain Points and Suggest Improvements Based on Feedback

In an e-commerce context, a company can leverage AI to analyze customer feedback from various channels such as surveys, product reviews, and support tickets. The AI system categorizes and identifies recurring themes and sentiment, such as issues with product quality, delivery delays, or customer service inefficiencies. By analyzing these patterns, AI can suggest specific improvements, such as enhancing the packaging, improving delivery tracking systems, or training customer support teams. Below is a sample dataset containing feedback and AI-driven insights for improving customer service.

Sample Feedback Data (Raw Feedback)

Customer ID	Feedback Type	Feedback
101	Survey	"The product arrived damaged and I had to wait too long for a replacement."
102	Review	"Great product, but delivery was slow and tracking didn't work."
103	Support Ticket	"Customer service was unhelpful when I had a question about my order."
104	Survey	"The packaging was poor, and the item was not as described."
105	Review	"Fast delivery, but the item was too small for my needs."

AI-Generated Insights and Suggestions

Customer ID	Identified Pain Point	AI Suggestion	Sentiment Score
101	Damaged product, slow replacement	Improve product packaging and logistics	Negative
102	Slow delivery, tracking issues	Enhance delivery tracking system	Negative
103	Unhelpful customer service	Train customer service for better support	Negative
104	Poor packaging, inaccurate item	Improve product description and packaging quality	Negative
105	Item too small	Provide better product size information	Neutral

Explanation and Interpretation of Results:

1. **Pain Points Identified:**
   o **Damaged Products:** Customers reported receiving damaged items (Customer 101). This could point to issues in packaging or handling.
   o **Slow Delivery & Tracking Issues:** Customers (102) expressed dissatisfaction with delayed deliveries and non-functional tracking.
   o **Unhelpful Customer Service:** One customer (103) highlighted a poor experience with customer support, suggesting the need for better training.
   o **Inaccurate Product Descriptions & Poor Packaging:** Customers (104) indicated that the product descriptions did not match the received product, and the packaging was subpar.
   o **Sizing Issues:** Customer 105 reported dissatisfaction with the size of the product, indicating that more detailed size charts or information is needed.

2. **AI Suggestions:**

   o **Packaging Improvements:** AI suggests enhancing packaging materials and practices to avoid damage during shipping (for example, reinforced boxes or better padding).

   o **Logistics & Delivery Enhancements:** AI recommends improving tracking systems and delivery timelines, potentially by collaborating with more reliable courier services.

   o **Customer Service Training:** AI suggests that customer support teams undergo further training to handle inquiries more efficiently and helpfully.

   o **Product Descriptions & Packaging Quality:** AI recommends ensuring that the online product descriptions are accurate and align with what customers will receive, and improving packaging quality.

   o **Size Information:** AI identifies that clearer product size information should be provided, possibly through more detailed charts or offering a size guide.

3. **Results Interpretation:**

   o The majority of feedback is negative, indicating customer dissatisfaction with various aspects of the shopping experience. The most significant issues seem to be delivery delays, damaged products, and inadequate customer service.

   o Neutral feedback (such as from Customer 105) highlights areas of potential improvement but does not necessarily point to strong dissatisfaction.

Decisions from the E-Commerce Perspective:

- **Operational Changes:** The company should prioritize improving packaging quality to prevent damages and explore partnerships with more reliable logistics providers to address slow delivery and tracking issues.

- **Customer Service Improvement:** Immediate investment in customer service training can improve satisfaction and resolve issues faster.

- **Product Information Clarity:** Providing clearer, more accurate product descriptions and size information will help reduce misunderstandings and returns.

- **Feedback Loop Implementation:** The company should set up a system to continually gather and analyze customer feedback to monitor the effectiveness of the changes made.

In summary, using AI to analyze customer feedback provides actionable insights that can drive significant improvements in the customer experience, leading to better retention, increased satisfaction, and ultimately higher sales.

10. AI for Customer Retention and Loyalty

AI has become a powerful tool in enhancing customer retention and loyalty, providing businesses with the ability to understand customer behavior more deeply. By analyzing vast amounts of data, AI can identify patterns in how customers interact with products and services.

This information allows companies to personalize their offerings, ensuring that each customer feels valued. For example, AI-driven algorithms can recommend products based on previous purchases or browsing history, making the shopping experience more tailored and engaging.

AI also helps in predicting future customer behavior. By utilizing predictive analytics, businesses can anticipate when a customer might be on the verge of leaving and take proactive steps to retain them. For instance, AI can detect a decline in a customer's engagement with the brand and trigger timely interventions, such as personalized offers or reminders, to keep them interested. This early identification of potential churn gives businesses the opportunity to act before it's too late.

Customer service is another area where AI plays a key role in boosting loyalty. With AI-powered chatbots and virtual assistants, companies can provide 24/7 support, ensuring that customers always have access to help when they need it. These systems can handle a variety of queries, from simple questions to more complex issues, offering fast and efficient resolutions. As a result, customers experience a seamless interaction with the brand, which fosters a sense of trust and reliability.

Furthermore, AI can enhance the overall customer experience by automating routine tasks, allowing human agents to focus on more complex interactions. This leads to faster response times and more personalized service. AI systems can also analyze customer feedback from various channels, providing valuable insights into customer sentiment. By understanding what customers appreciate and what needs improvement, businesses can adapt their strategies to meet customer expectations more effectively.

AI can also support loyalty programs by making them more engaging and rewarding. Through machine learning, companies can identify which rewards or incentives are most appealing to specific customers. This allows businesses to create more targeted loyalty offers, making customers feel more appreciated and incentivized to continue their relationship with the brand. Personalized loyalty rewards can increase the likelihood of repeat purchases and long-term engagement, which is crucial for building brand loyalty.

In addition to these benefits, AI can continuously learn and improve its understanding of customers over time. As it gathers more data, it becomes better at predicting customer needs and preferences, allowing businesses to refine their strategies even further. By maintaining an ongoing cycle of data collection, analysis, and adjustment, AI helps companies build stronger, more loyal customer relationships that can lead to sustained business growth.

Practical Example of AI for Customer Retention and Loyalty:

An e-commerce company uses AI-powered predictive analytics to enhance customer retention and loyalty. The AI model analyzes customer behavior, purchase history, and interaction patterns to predict which customers are most likely to churn (stop making purchases). It also segments customers based on their purchasing patterns, frequency, and lifetime value to deliver personalized recommendations, discounts, or loyalty rewards.

Sample Data:

Customer ID	Purchase Frequency (Last 6 Months)	Average Order Value ($)	Lifetime Value ($)	Churn Probability (%)	Loyalty Program Status	Predicted Next Purchase (Days)
1001	5	150	1200	5%	Active	10
1002	2	80	350	60%	Inactive	30
1003	8	200	1800	2%	Active	7
1004	1	50	250	80%	Inactive	60
1005	4	120	800	30%	Active	14

Output and Results Interpretation:

- **Churn Probability**: Customers with higher churn probability (e.g., Customer 1002 and Customer 1004) are at risk of leaving, and they could be targeted with retention strategies such as personalized offers or re-engagement emails.

- **Purchase Frequency**: Customers with higher purchase frequency (e.g., Customer 1003) are less likely to churn and are more loyal. They may benefit from loyalty rewards like exclusive offers or early access to sales.

- **Loyalty Program Status**: Customers marked as "Inactive" (e.g., Customer 1002 and Customer 1004) may need extra attention to encourage engagement with the loyalty program.

- **Predicted Next Purchase**: Shorter prediction intervals (e.g., Customer 1003 with 7 days) indicate that these customers are more likely to make a purchase soon, whereas longer intervals (e.g., Customer 1004 with 60 days) indicate that these customers are less engaged and may need targeted outreach.

Observations:

1. **Customer Segmentation**: The AI model segments customers into high, medium, and low engagement groups based on purchase

frequency and churn probability. This enables personalized strategies.

2. **Targeted Actions**: Customers with high churn probabilities or lower engagement can be targeted with retention tactics like discounts or reminders about loyalty benefits.

3. **Loyalty Program Optimization**: For customers who are inactive in the loyalty program, incentives or exclusive offers can be used to reignite interest and increase their engagement.

E-Commerce Decisions:

1. **Retention Campaigns**: Focus on customers with high churn probabilities, offering discounts, personalized communication, or loyalty program reactivation.

2. **Upsell and Cross-sell**: For high-value customers (e.g., Customer 1003), provide recommendations or exclusive offers based on their purchasing behavior to further increase their lifetime value.

3. **Personalized Rewards**: Tailor loyalty rewards for each customer segment. Active customers may get early access to new products, while inactive ones may be offered a re-engagement incentive.

By using AI for customer retention, the e-commerce company can significantly improve its customer loyalty and reduce churn by making informed, data-driven decisions.

10.1 Predicting Customer Churn with AI

Customer churn refers to the loss of clients or customers who stop doing business with a company over a specific period. Predicting churn is critical for businesses to maintain their customer base, reduce attrition, and identify areas that need improvement. Artificial intelligence (AI) has revolutionized this process by offering tools that can analyze vast amounts of customer data to forecast which individuals are most likely to leave. AI can process customer behavior patterns, transaction histories, and engagement metrics, helping businesses spot early warning signs of potential churn.

AI models are trained on historical data, where customer interactions, such as purchase history, complaints, and customer support interactions, are examined. By understanding how previous customers interacted with the company before leaving, AI can create a predictive model that highlights the risk factors for current customers. This allows businesses to focus their retention efforts on high-risk customers, offering personalized incentives or interventions to keep them engaged and satisfied.

One of the significant advantages of using AI for churn prediction is its ability to detect complex patterns in data that may not be immediately obvious to human analysts. For instance, AI can recognize subtle changes in customer behavior, such as a drop in purchase frequency or a slowdown in website visits, which might indicate an increased risk of churn. These insights can be valuable for decision-makers to take proactive steps before a customer decides to leave.

AI models also continually improve over time. As more data is collected, the models become more accurate at predicting churn. This iterative learning process allows AI systems to adapt to changing customer preferences and market conditions. Unlike traditional models that might require manual updates or recalibration, AI can autonomously refine its predictions, leading to more effective retention strategies over the long term.

Furthermore, businesses can use AI-driven churn predictions in various ways. For example, marketing teams can craft targeted campaigns for at-risk customers, while customer service teams can provide tailored support to resolve specific issues. AI can also inform pricing strategies or product recommendations, ensuring that businesses offer solutions that address individual customer needs and prevent churn.

Incorporating AI for churn prediction leads to better resource allocation. Instead of spending time and money on broad retention efforts, businesses can focus on the customers who are most likely to leave, making the process more efficient. As a result, companies can improve customer satisfaction, reduce churn, and ultimately enhance profitability by leveraging AI to understand and address the factors that drive customers away.

Practical Example Context:

In an e-commerce business, customer retention is a crucial factor for sustaining long-term growth. By using predictive models to identify customers likely to churn, the company can proactively target them with retention strategies, such as personalized offers or discounts. In this example, we are using customer behavior and transaction data to predict which customers are likely to stop purchasing from the platform. We use various features, such as purchase frequency, total spending, time since last purchase, and customer satisfaction score to build the churn prediction model. The model outputs a probability of churn for each customer.

Sample Customer Data:

Customer ID	Age	Purchase Frequency (per month)	Total Spend (last 6 months)	Days Since Last Purchase	Satisfaction Score (1-10)	Churn Probability (%)
C001	30	3	500	10	8	15
C002	45	1	100	50	5	75
C003	26	5	1200	2	9	10
C004	60	0	0	90	3	90
C005	33	2	300	20	7	30
C006	40	4	700	15	6	40

Churn Prediction Model Output and Results:

From the predictive model, we obtain the churn probability for each customer. These values reflect the likelihood that each customer will churn, with higher percentages indicating a higher likelihood of leaving.

Interpretation of Results:

- **Customer C001 (Churn Probability: 15%)**: This customer has a moderate churn probability. With a high satisfaction score and frequent purchases, this customer is less likely to churn but may benefit from a loyalty program to further encourage engagement.

- **Customer C002 (Churn Probability: 75%)**: This customer is highly likely to churn. The low purchase frequency, low total spend, and a significant gap since the last purchase indicate that the customer is not actively engaged. A targeted retention strategy, such as offering a discount or special offer, may help prevent churn.

- **Customer C003 (Churn Probability: 10%)**: This customer has a low churn probability, making them a valuable customer. Their frequent purchases and high satisfaction score suggest they are satisfied, and no immediate action may be necessary.

- **Customer C004 (Churn Probability: 90%)**: This customer is almost certain to churn, with no recent purchases and a very low satisfaction score. A re-engagement campaign or exit survey may help understand their reasons for leaving.

- **Customer C005 (Churn Probability: 30%)**: This customer shows a moderate churn risk. Although they haven't made purchases frequently, the moderate satisfaction score suggests they could be retained with the right incentives.

- **Customer C006 (Churn Probability: 40%)**: This customer is at a moderate risk of churning. Their spending is relatively high, but their satisfaction score is low. A targeted intervention might help improve their experience and retention.

Observations:

1. **High churn risk is correlated with low purchase frequency and low satisfaction scores**. Customers with fewer recent purchases and lower satisfaction are more likely to leave.

2. **Proactive measures**: The company should focus on customers with higher churn probabilities (like C002, C004, and C006) by offering discounts or special incentives to encourage them to stay.

3. **Loyalty programs**: Customers with moderate churn risk or lower probabilities (like C001 and C003) could benefit from loyalty programs or exclusive offers to improve retention and increase lifetime value.

Decisions from the E-Commerce Perspective:

- **Targeted Marketing Campaigns**: Based on churn probabilities, customers like C002 and C004 should be prioritized for special offers or customer retention campaigns.

- **Personalized Offers**: Offering tailored discounts or personalized recommendations to customers at moderate risk (C005, C006) may improve their retention and loyalty.

- **Enhancing Customer Experience**: Improving the satisfaction scores of customers at high risk of churn, through improved service, better product recommendations, or personalized interactions, can reduce churn.

- **Regular Monitoring**: Continuously updating the predictive model with fresh data will ensure the business stays ahead of customer behavior trends and can make timely adjustments to retention strategies.

10.2 Personalized Loyalty Programs Powered by AI

Personalized loyalty programs powered by AI have transformed the way businesses interact with their customers. With AI technology, companies can gather and analyze vast amounts of customer data, such as purchase history, browsing behavior, and social media activity. This information allows businesses to create tailored loyalty experiences that resonate with individual preferences, making customers feel valued and understood. By utilizing AI, brands can identify patterns and predict future behaviors, allowing for more relevant and engaging loyalty rewards and offers.

AI-driven personalization enables businesses to provide dynamic rewards, adjusting them based on a customer's engagement and spending habits. For instance, a customer who frequently purchases certain products may receive discounts on similar items or exclusive offers related to their interests. This approach not only increases the likelihood of repeat purchases but also fosters a deeper emotional connection between the brand and the customer. By using AI to continuously monitor and adapt the loyalty program, businesses can keep customers engaged and loyal over time.

The use of AI in loyalty programs can also help streamline customer communication. Automated, personalized messages can be sent to customers at the right moment, such as when they are nearing a reward milestone or when there are exclusive promotions available. These interactions are highly customized and feel more personal, making customers more likely to engage with the program. Additionally, AI can predict the best time to reach out to each individual, ensuring that messages are sent when they are most likely to be seen and acted upon.

AI-powered loyalty programs also benefit businesses by increasing customer retention and reducing churn. By offering tailored experiences, brands can create a sense of exclusivity and value that encourages customers to stay loyal. Over time, this results in a more dedicated customer base, which can be highly profitable. The ability to anticipate customer needs and deliver relevant rewards helps ensure that customers feel appreciated, leading them to stay with the brand longer and spend more money over time.

Moreover, AI allows for the creation of multi-channel loyalty programs that provide seamless experiences across various platforms, such as mobile apps, websites, and in-store. Customers can engage with the program in whichever way is most convenient for them, with their data being integrated across all touchpoints. This flexibility enhances customer satisfaction and encourages greater participation in the loyalty program, as customers can interact with it in ways that fit their lifestyles.

In the long run, AI-driven personalized loyalty programs provide businesses with a competitive edge. As customers become accustomed to receiving personalized rewards and interactions, they will begin to expect this level of customization from other brands as well. Companies that adopt AI for their loyalty programs will not only retain a more loyal customer base but will also position themselves as innovative and customer-focused, which can help them stand out in a crowded marketplace.

Practical Example:

An e-commerce company wants to enhance its customer loyalty program by using AI to personalize offers based on customer preferences and purchase history. By analyzing the past behavior of customers (such as frequent purchases, preferred categories, and spending habits), the system can automatically generate personalized rewards and discounts. The company uses machine learning to segment customers into different categories based on their purchasing patterns, and offers tailored rewards to increase engagement. For example, customers who frequently buy fashion-related items might receive discounts on new clothing lines, while those who buy home goods might get rewards on related items.

Sample Data:

Customer ID	Name	Total Spend	Frequent Categories	Last Purchase Date	Loyalty Tier	Suggested Offer
001	John Doe	$1200	Fashion, Electronics	2025-01-12	Gold	15% off on Fashion & Tech
002	Jane Smith	$450	Home Goods, Beauty	2024-12-30	Silver	10% off on Home & Beauty
003	Sam Lee	$800	Books, Office Supplies	2025-01-10	Gold	12% off on Books & Office

Customer ID	Name	Total Spend	Frequent Categories	Last Purchase Date	Loyalty Tier	Suggested Offer
004	Alice Green	$350	Grocery, Kitchenware	2024-12-22	Bronze	5% off on Kitchen & Grocery
005	Mark Black	$2200	Fashion, Travel, Sports	2025-01-08	Platinum	20% off on Fashion & Sports

Output and Results:

1. **Customer Segmentation:** Based on total spend and purchase history, the customers are segmented into different loyalty tiers— Platinum, Gold, Silver, and Bronze.

2. **Offer Personalization:** Tailored offers are generated based on the frequent categories for each customer. For example, John Doe, who buys both Fashion and Electronics, receives an offer on both categories.

3. **Engagement Opportunities:** The system identifies customers like Mark Black (Platinum tier) who are high spenders across multiple categories, offering them more exclusive discounts to retain loyalty.

4. **Product Promotions:** Customers with specific preferences, such as Alice Green, who frequently buys kitchenware, receive discounts tailored to those categories.

Explanation and Interpretation of Results:

- **Personalization Drives Engagement:** Customers in higher tiers (Platinum/Gold) are likely to respond well to larger, category-specific discounts, which incentivize them to continue shopping.

- **Targeting Based on Behavior:** John Doe and Sam Lee, for instance, receive tailored offers based on their unique preferences (Fashion, Tech, Books), showing that AI can recommend deals more aligned with customer interests, potentially increasing conversion rates.

- **Tier-Based Incentives:** Higher-spending customers (like Mark Black) are offered larger discounts, reinforcing their loyalty to the brand and encouraging bigger purchases in the future.

- **Budget Management:** Smaller discounts for lower-tier customers (like Alice Green) ensure the business doesn't over-discount on lower-value transactions, maintaining profitability.

Observations:

- Customers with higher total spend tend to receive more significant discounts, which aligns with the strategy of rewarding loyal and high-value customers.

- AI-driven personalization helps in identifying relevant offers for customers based on their purchase patterns, leading to a more customer-centric experience.

- The data-driven approach optimizes loyalty program spending by focusing resources on high-potential customers (Platinum and Gold), ensuring the business maximizes return on investment.

Decisions from the E-Commerce Perspective:

1. **Optimize Loyalty Tiers:** Ensure that the loyalty program is clearly differentiated across spending levels to maximize the value of rewards.

2. **Increase Cross-Selling Opportunities:** Based on customer preferences, the business should bundle related items (e.g., fashion + electronics) to increase overall cart size.

3. **Track Offer Effectiveness:** Continuously monitor the success rate of personalized offers and adjust the discounts or incentives based on customer response and purchase frequency.

10.3 Retention Strategies and AI-Driven Engagement

Retention strategies focus on keeping customers engaged and loyal to a brand, as it's often more cost-effective to retain existing customers than acquire new ones. To do this, companies need to understand the factors that influence customer satisfaction and loyalty, such as product quality, customer service, and personalized experiences. Offering rewards, loyalty programs, and regular communication helps create a connection that encourages customers to return. Additionally, gathering customer feedback and continuously improving products or services can foster long-term relationships.

AI-driven engagement has become a key tool in enhancing retention strategies. By leveraging artificial intelligence, businesses can analyze vast amounts of customer data to gain insights into behaviors and preferences. This information allows them to create personalized experiences that resonate with individual customers, making them feel valued. For example, AI can recommend products based on past purchases or browsing behavior, increasing the chances of repeat business.

Moreover, AI can enhance customer service through chatbots and virtual assistants, which are available 24/7. These tools can instantly address customer inquiries, resolve issues, and guide users through the purchasing process. With AI, the customer experience becomes more efficient and tailored, which leads to higher satisfaction and retention. The ability to predict and proactively address customer concerns further deepens the relationship and reduces the likelihood of churn.

Incorporating AI also allows for more dynamic communication strategies. AI-powered tools can automate personalized emails, messages, or promotions at just the right time based on customer behavior. This level of precision improves customer engagement and encourages them to stay loyal to the brand. By automating repetitive tasks, businesses can allocate their resources to more strategic efforts while still maintaining a high level of personalization.

Another benefit of AI in retention strategies is its ability to analyze customer feedback in real-time. Sentiment analysis tools can detect changes in customer satisfaction and help companies act quickly to address any issues before they result in churn. By keeping a pulse on customer sentiment, businesses can continually adjust their strategies and improve the overall customer experience.

Ultimately, the combination of AI-driven insights and customer-centric strategies creates a powerful approach to retention. By personalizing experiences, anticipating needs, and delivering exceptional service, businesses can increase the likelihood of customers returning time and again. Retention isn't just about keeping customers around; it's about creating genuine value and fostering long-lasting relationships that benefit both the customer and the company.

Practical Example:

In an e-commerce environment, businesses often use AI to analyze customer behavior and send personalized offers or discounts to increase retention. By using AI algorithms to evaluate past purchasing patterns, preferences, and engagement data, companies can identify the best time and type of offer to send to each customer. This personalization increases the likelihood of repeat purchases, improving customer loyalty and retention.

Sample Data:

Customer ID	Age	Gender	Total Spend (Last 6 Months)	Purchase Frequency	Product Category Purchased	Last Purchase Date	Average Spend Per Purchase	Personalized Offer Sent
1001	35	Female	$500	5	Fashion	2024-12-01	$100	20% off on Fashion items
1002	42	Male	$1,000	8	Electronics	2024-12-10	$125	15% off on Electronics
1003	28	Female	$200	3	Beauty	2024-11-28	$66.67	10% off on Beauty items

Customer ID	Age	Gender	Total Spend (Last 6 Months)	Purchase Frequency	Product Category Purchased	Last Purchase Date	Average Spend Per Purchase	Personalized Offer Sent
1004	55	Male	$1,500	12	Home & Kitchen	2024-12-05	$125	25% off on Home & Kitchen
1005	30	Female	$350	6	Sports	2024-12-08	$58.33	15% off on Sports items

Output and Results:

- **Personalized Offers Sent:**
    - **Customer 1001:** Based on her purchase history in fashion and moderate spending, a **20% off offer** for fashion items was sent to encourage further engagement.
    - **Customer 1002:** A frequent shopper with higher spending in electronics was given a **15% off on electronics** to reinforce his purchasing habits in this category.
    - **Customer 1003:** With fewer total purchases and lower spend, a **10% off on beauty items** was targeted to increase her purchase frequency.
    - **Customer 1004:** A highly engaged customer with high spending, especially in home & kitchen items, was given a **25% off on home & kitchen** to reward loyalty and drive repeat purchases.
    - **Customer 1005:** A moderately frequent shopper in the sports category was offered a **15% off on sports items** to encourage a higher spend per purchase.

Observations:

1. **Personalized offers align with purchase history:** The AI uses the customer's most frequently purchased categories to target them with

offers that are likely to convert. For instance, a customer who frequently purchases fashion items is more likely to respond positively to a fashion-related offer.

2. **Discount levels are adjusted to customer behavior:** Customers with higher spending or frequent purchases receive larger discounts, reflecting their loyalty and engagement.

3. **Customer retention is likely to increase:** Customers are more likely to return when they feel their needs and preferences are understood, as the offers are tailored to their specific purchasing behavior.

Interpretation and Decisions from an E-commerce Perspective:

- **Effective Personalization:** The AI-driven system has successfully segmented customers based on their preferences, behavior, and spending patterns. Offers were tailored to align with each customer's interests, improving the chance of purchase.

- **Higher Discounts for Loyal Customers:** Offering larger discounts to high-spending and frequent customers (like Customer 1004) helps reinforce their loyalty and encourages repeat purchases, while lower discounts can be used to increase engagement from less frequent buyers (e.g., Customer 1003).

- **Optimizing for Customer Segments:** By analyzing purchase categories and customer preferences, the e-commerce business can develop further segments (e.g., "high spenders," "occasional shoppers," etc.) to offer more precise discounts, thus increasing overall customer retention.

Decisions for E-commerce Growth:

1. **Segment Marketing:** Continue using AI to refine customer segmentation and send personalized offers based on real-time data, enhancing customer experience and driving engagement.

2. **Discount Strategy:** Consider adjusting discount levels and types based on customer loyalty and purchase behavior, ensuring offers resonate with the most valuable customers.

3. **Cross-selling and Upselling:** Use the data to cross-sell or upsell related items to customers based on their previous purchases (e.g., sending offers for accessories when a customer buys a fashion item).

11. AI for Marketing Analytics

AI in marketing analytics is transforming the way businesses understand and engage with their customers. By analyzing large sets of data, AI tools can uncover patterns and trends that would be nearly impossible for humans to detect manually. This allows companies to gain deeper insights into customer behavior, preferences, and purchase decisions.

The ability to predict what customers might do next or how they might respond to certain campaigns can significantly enhance decision-making and lead to more targeted marketing strategies.

AI helps businesses optimize their marketing campaigns by identifying the most effective messaging and delivery channels. For instance, AI can track which ads, emails, or social media posts generate the best engagement and conversions. With this information, marketers can adjust their strategies in real time to improve the overall effectiveness of their campaigns. AI-powered tools also allow for personalized marketing, where content is tailored to the unique needs and interests of individual customers, increasing the likelihood of conversions.

AI technologies like machine learning can help businesses segment their audience more accurately. Instead of relying on broad demographic data, AI can segment customers based on behaviors, past interactions, and buying patterns. This leads to more precise targeting, ensuring that marketing efforts are reaching the right people with the right message. By making these segments smaller and more specific, AI enables a more personalized approach that resonates with each group's unique needs and desires.

Another significant benefit of AI in marketing analytics is its ability to automate repetitive tasks, saving marketers time and resources. AI can handle data collection, analysis, and even reporting, allowing marketing teams to focus on more strategic and creative tasks. Automation also reduces the risk of human error and ensures that data is processed consistently and accurately. This means that marketers can spend less time on manual data handling and more time on designing campaigns that drive results.

Predictive analytics is another area where AI plays a vital role in marketing. By analyzing historical data, AI can forecast future trends, consumer behavior, and market conditions. This can give companies a competitive edge, as they can plan and adjust their strategies ahead of time. Whether it's predicting customer churn or forecasting demand for certain products, AI helps businesses make informed decisions and prepare for what lies ahead, rather than reacting to events as they happen.

Lastly, AI helps marketers measure and track the effectiveness of their campaigns with greater precision. It can provide real-time insights into how a campaign is performing across various channels and touchpoints, allowing for quick adjustments if something isn't working. This level of monitoring ensures that resources are being spent efficiently and that campaigns are delivering the best possible ROI. By continuously analyzing results, AI can also suggest improvements, helping businesses to constantly refine their marketing efforts and stay ahead of the competition.

Practical Example: AI for Marketing Analytics in E-Commerce

A popular e-commerce company is looking to optimize its marketing campaigns using AI-based predictive analytics to improve customer retention. The goal is to analyze historical customer data to predict the likelihood of customers making repeat purchases within 30 days after their first purchase. The marketing team will use these insights to target high-potential customers with tailored promotions to increase sales.

Sample Data:

Customer ID	First Purchase Date	Total Spend	Visit Frequency (per month)	Days Since Last Purchase	Predicted Probability of Repeat Purchase (%)
001	2024-12-01	$150	5	15	80
002	2024-12-10	$200	4	7	60
003	2024-12-15	$80	3	30	40
004	2024-11-30	$220	6	5	90
005	2024-12-20	$50	2	20	30

Output & Results:

The AI model was trained on historical data to predict the likelihood of repeat purchases. Based on the predictions:

- **Customer 001** has an 80% probability of making a repeat purchase. With a high total spend and frequent visits, they are likely to engage with a follow-up promotion.

- **Customer 002** has a 60% chance, indicating moderate likelihood of return, influenced by a recent purchase and a fairly high total spend.

- **Customer 003** shows only a 40% chance of returning, as their recent purchase is 30 days old, and they have a lower frequency of visits.

- **Customer 004** is highly likely to return, with a 90% probability, due to recent activity and high engagement.

- **Customer 005** has only a 30% probability, reflecting their low frequency of visits and the smaller spend.

Interpretation & Observations:

- **High Probability:** Customers like **001** and **004** have high engagement levels and are likely to respond well to follow-up promotions or personalized offers.

- **Moderate Probability:** Customers such as **002** may require additional attention, such as targeted discounts or personalized content to encourage repeat visits.

- **Low Probability:** Customers like **003** and **005** show lower chances of returning. Retargeting efforts may need to be stronger, or it might be more cost-effective to focus on higher-potential customers.

E-Commerce Perspective Decisions:

- **Targeting Strategy:** Focus marketing resources on **high probability customers (001 and 004)** for retargeting with exclusive promotions and offers. These customers are more likely to respond positively.

- **Personalization:** For **moderate probability customers (002)**, consider personalized follow-up emails or discounts tailored to their past behaviors (e.g., product recommendations based on their total spend).

- **Retargeting Campaigns:** For **low probability customers (003 and 005)**, consider offering incentives to encourage further purchases, but avoid overspending on these groups. Alternative strategies, like re-engagement campaigns (e.g., reminder emails with discounts), might be used.

By using AI-driven insights, the marketing team can focus their efforts more efficiently, maximizing the return on investment for their marketing campaigns and improving overall customer retention.

11.1 AI-Powered Marketing Attribution Models

AI-powered marketing attribution models are designed to help businesses understand the impact of various marketing activities on customer behavior and conversions. Traditional attribution models, such as first-touch or last-touch attribution, only give a limited view by focusing on one point of interaction along the customer journey. AI-driven models, however, use advanced algorithms to track the entire journey, from initial awareness to final purchase, providing a more comprehensive and accurate view of how different marketing channels contribute to success.

These models leverage machine learning techniques to analyze vast amounts of data collected from multiple touchpoints, such as websites, social media, email campaigns, and paid ads. By processing this data, AI models can identify patterns, trends, and relationships between customer actions and marketing efforts. This allows businesses to understand which channels are most effective and how various interactions influence each other, even if they occur at different stages of the customer journey.

One of the key advantages of AI-powered attribution is its ability to handle complex, multi-channel marketing campaigns. Unlike traditional models that might give credit to just one or two touchpoints, AI models can assign fractional credit across all touchpoints based on their contribution. This provides marketers with a much clearer picture of how each piece of their marketing strategy works together to drive conversions, enabling more informed decision-making and optimized resource allocation.

Additionally, AI models continually improve over time. They are capable of learning from new data and adapting to changing market conditions, consumer behaviors, and marketing trends. This means that the attribution model evolves with the business, ensuring that the insights provided remain relevant and accurate as the marketing landscape shifts. It also allows marketers to test different strategies and see real-time results, making it easier to adjust campaigns for better performance.

Despite their advantages, AI-powered attribution models can be complex to implement and require significant data infrastructure. Businesses must ensure that they have access to accurate and comprehensive data across all their marketing channels. Moreover, the models need to be properly calibrated to avoid potential biases in data interpretation, as incorrect or incomplete data could lead to inaccurate conclusions and suboptimal decision-making.

Overall, AI-powered marketing attribution offers businesses a powerful tool to understand the true effectiveness of their marketing efforts. By moving beyond simplistic models and embracing data-driven insights, companies can enhance their strategies, improve ROI, and gain a competitive edge in a crowded market. However, success with these models depends on the quality of the data, the sophistication of the AI system, and the ability of marketers to interpret the insights effectively.

Practical Example:

An e-commerce company is running a marketing campaign across several channels, including Google Ads, Facebook Ads, and Email marketing. The company uses AI to track sales and attribute them to the respective marketing channels, aiming to identify which channel is performing best in driving conversions. The data used includes marketing spend, the number of impressions, clicks, and the total sales generated. The goal is to optimize marketing efforts and budget allocation.

Sample Marketing Campaign Data:

Channel	Marketing Spend ($)	Impressions	Clicks	Conversion Rate (%)	Total Sales ($)
Google Ads	5,000	500,000	25,000	5	12,500
Facebook Ads	4,000	300,000	12,000	4	8,000
Email Marketing	2,000	100,000	5,000	10	15,000

AI Attribution Model Output:

Channel	Attributed Sales ($)	Attribution Weight (%)	ROI ($)
Google Ads	11,000	44%	2.2
Facebook Ads	6,500	26%	1.6
Email Marketing	13,000	52%	7.5

Interpretation of Results:

- **Google Ads**: With $5,000 spent, Google Ads generated $12,500 in total sales. However, the AI attribution model assigns $11,000 in attributed sales, accounting for 44% of the total attributed sales across all channels. The ROI of 2.2 shows a decent return on investment.

- **Facebook Ads**: Facebook Ads generated $8,000 in sales with $4,000 in spend, but the AI model attributed $6,500 in sales, indicating that Facebook contributed less effectively than Google Ads in terms of conversion despite a higher proportion of impressions. The ROI of 1.6 is lower than Google Ads, indicating a lower return.

- **Email Marketing**: Email marketing had the highest ROI of 7.5 with an attributed sales amount of $13,000 from a $2,000 spend, indicating it was the most effective channel in terms of return on investment, with a 52% share of the attributed sales.

Decisions from an E-Commerce Perspective:

1. **Budget Allocation**: Given that Email Marketing offers the highest ROI and share of attributed sales, the company should consider allocating a larger portion of the marketing budget to email campaigns. Despite Facebook Ads having a larger spend, its ROI is significantly lower, signaling a need for optimization or potential reassessment of this channel.

2. **Optimization of Google Ads**: Since Google Ads has a strong contribution (44%) and ROI (2.2), it remains an effective channel, but there is room for optimization to further reduce costs and increase conversions.

3. **Re-evaluation of Facebook Ads**: With Facebook Ads showing a lower ROI (1.6), the company should re-evaluate its targeting strategy, ad creatives, and possibly explore more focused ad placements to improve its performance.

4. **Channel Expansion**: If the company considers expanding its efforts, channels similar to Email Marketing (e.g., newsletters, loyalty programs) could be prioritized to increase customer retention and boost conversions without significantly increasing spend.

The use of AI in attributing sales to specific channels allows the company to make data-driven decisions, optimize their budget allocation, and focus on high-performing channels while reevaluating or adjusting less effective ones.

11.2 Customer Journey Mapping with AI

Customer journey mapping with AI involves using advanced algorithms to understand and visualize the interactions a customer has with a business from the first point of contact to the final purchase. It aims to capture the complete experience, identifying each touchpoint where the customer engages with the brand. AI analyzes vast amounts of data to pinpoint trends, preferences, and pain points that may not be immediately obvious through traditional methods. This approach allows businesses to gain deeper insights into customer behavior, improving overall service and communication.

AI-driven customer journey mapping starts by collecting data from various channels, such as social media, email interactions, website visits, and in-store experiences. Machine learning models can sift through this data to identify patterns and segment customers based on their behaviors and preferences. With this wealth of information, businesses can map out how customers move through different stages, providing a clearer picture of the entire journey. The result is a more personalized experience for each customer, as the business can now address their specific needs at every stage.

As customers engage with a brand, AI tools can track and predict their next moves, using predictive analytics to anticipate their actions. For example, if a customer frequently browses a specific product but hasn't yet made a purchase, AI can trigger personalized recommendations or discounts at the right moment. This predictive capability allows companies to respond in real time, guiding the customer toward conversion in a way that feels natural and helpful. It also ensures that the customer journey is optimized for efficiency, making each interaction more relevant and engaging.

One of the key advantages of AI in journey mapping is the ability to personalize interactions at scale. While traditional methods might rely on general assumptions about customer behavior, AI can tailor experiences based on individual data. This could include customized offers, targeted messaging, and content that resonates with the customer's preferences. Personalization helps build stronger relationships between the brand and its customers, increasing customer loyalty and satisfaction over time. The more AI learns about a customer's unique journey, the better it can refine its recommendations and actions.

AI also helps businesses detect and address issues in the customer journey that could lead to dissatisfaction or abandonment. Through sentiment analysis and real-time feedback monitoring, AI can identify negative experiences or roadblocks in the customer journey, such as slow website load times or confusing checkout processes. By addressing these issues proactively, businesses can improve the overall customer experience, reducing the risk of lost sales and enhancing customer retention. The faster a company can identify and fix problems, the more likely they are to maintain customer trust.

Finally, AI-driven customer journey mapping not only benefits customers but also enables businesses to make data-driven decisions that improve their strategies. By analyzing the effectiveness of various touchpoints and channels, companies can adjust their marketing and customer service efforts. AI provides the insights needed to optimize resource allocation, ensuring that the business invests in the areas that yield the greatest return. Over time, this continuous feedback loop enables businesses to refine their approach, making customer journey mapping an invaluable tool for long-term success.

Practical Example:

Imagine an e-commerce company using AI to visualize and optimize the customer journey from acquisition to purchase. The company collects data from various touchpoints like website visits, product interactions, cart abandonment, and purchase completions. By analyzing these touchpoints, AI helps identify patterns, bottlenecks, and opportunities for improvement in the customer journey. The goal is to improve conversion rates by better understanding customer behaviors, preferences, and pain points.

Sample Customer Interaction Data:

Customer ID	Acquisition Channel	Product View	Add to Cart	Checkout Started	Purchase Completed	Time to Purchase (Days)	Conversion Rate (%)
001	Social Media	5	2	Yes	Yes	2	40%
002	Organic Search	3	1	No	No	0	0%
003	Email Marketing	6	3	Yes	Yes	1	50%
004	Paid Ads	8	5	Yes	No	5	20%

Customer ID	Acquisition Channel	Product View	Added to Cart	Checkout Started	Purchase Completed	Time to Purchase (Days)	Conversion Rate (%)
005	Referral	4	2	No	No	0	0%

Output and Results:

1. **Acquisition Channel Performance:**

   o Customers from **Email Marketing** show the highest conversion rate at 50%.

   o **Social Media** customers show a relatively good conversion rate of 40%, but **Paid Ads** customers are less likely to convert (20%).

   o **Organic Search** and **Referral** show zero conversions, indicating a need for improvement in those channels.

2. **Time to Purchase:**

   o Customers who complete the purchase within 1–2 days (like customers 003 and 001) have higher conversion rates compared to those who take longer or abandon the process.

3. **Bottlenecks Identified:**

   o **Checkout Abandonment:** Customers 004 and 002 added products to the cart but never completed the checkout. This indicates friction in the checkout process.

   o **Product View to Add to Cart:** The drop-off rate is higher from product views to adding to the cart, especially for customers from **Paid Ads** (5 product views but only 5 added to cart).

Interpretation:

- **Email Marketing** is an effective channel for conversions, likely due to a more personalized approach, which can be leveraged more.

- **Social Media** and **Paid Ads** show promise but need improvements in targeting and engagement strategies to reduce drop-offs.

- **Paid Ads** may need to better capture interest at the top of the funnel to ensure conversions as customers seem to engage with multiple products but fail to complete the purchase.

- **Checkout abandonment** points to the need for simplifying or improving the checkout process, perhaps by introducing clearer calls to action, removing unnecessary steps, or offering better payment options.

E-Commerce Perspective Decisions:

1. **Optimize Paid Ad Targeting:** Improve ad targeting and relevance by using AI insights to focus on products that appeal to the audience, reducing product-view-to-cart drop-offs.

2. **Enhance the Checkout Experience:** Focus on reducing friction during checkout, like offering guest checkout, minimizing form fields, and ensuring a mobile-friendly design.

3. **Maximize Email Marketing Impact:** Use AI to segment customer data for personalized email campaigns that address pain points and highlight relevant products, improving the already high conversion rate of 50%.

4. **Improve Organic Search and Referral Conversions:** Analyze search engine optimization (SEO) and referral strategies to increase visibility and ensure these channels lead to better conversions.

11.3 Predictive Analytics for Marketing Campaigns

Predictive analytics in marketing campaigns involves the use of data, statistical algorithms, and machine learning techniques to forecast future outcomes based on historical data. By analyzing trends and patterns in consumer behavior, businesses can predict which customers are most likely to respond to a particular marketing campaign. This approach helps marketers make data-driven decisions that increase the likelihood of success and improve return on investment (ROI).

One of the key benefits of predictive analytics is its ability to segment audiences effectively. By identifying characteristics of consumers who have previously responded to similar campaigns, businesses can tailor their marketing strategies to specific groups, ensuring messages are more relevant and personalized. This level of precision allows for more targeted campaigns, reducing waste and improving engagement rates.

Additionally, predictive analytics can help businesses anticipate customer behavior and optimize their strategies accordingly. For instance, by analyzing previous interactions, businesses can predict when a customer is likely to make a purchase or abandon a shopping cart. With this information, marketers can send timely reminders or special offers, improving conversion rates and customer retention.

Moreover, predictive analytics can enhance campaign performance by allowing businesses to allocate resources more effectively. By predicting which channels or tactics will yield the highest engagement, marketers can focus their efforts on the most promising avenues. This ensures that time, money, and effort are spent on the campaigns that are most likely to drive results, leading to a more efficient marketing budget.

Predictive models can also be used to forecast customer lifetime value (CLV), which helps businesses understand the long-term value of acquiring and retaining specific customers. By identifying high-value customers early on, marketers can prioritize building stronger relationships with these individuals, potentially leading to higher customer loyalty and repeat business. This focus on high-value prospects can significantly impact a company's growth and profitability.

Lastly, predictive analytics offers the advantage of continuous learning and improvement. As more data becomes available and marketing campaigns evolve, predictive models can be adjusted to reflect new patterns and trends. This iterative process ensures that marketing strategies remain effective over time, allowing businesses to stay ahead of their competitors and continually optimize their efforts for the best possible outcomes.

Practical Example:

A company runs several marketing campaigns each quarter for its e-commerce platform. They want to predict the success of future campaigns based on the performance of previous ones. AI models, specifically machine learning, can analyze historical data such as ad spend, engagement, conversion rates, and customer demographics to predict the success of upcoming campaigns. The company uses the past campaign data to train an AI model, which can then forecast the effectiveness of new campaigns, helping the marketing team make data-driven decisions on budget allocation, targeting, and strategy.

Sample Data on Past Campaigns:

Campaign ID	Ad Spend ($)	Clicks	Conversions	Conversion Rate (%)	Revenue ($)	Customer Demographics (Age Group)	Time of Year
1	500	800	100	12.5	1500	18-34	Summer
2	700	1200	150	12.5	2500	25-44	Fall
3	300	600	50	8.33	800	35-54	Winter
4	1000	1500	200	13.33	4000	18-34	Spring
5	400	700	70	10	1400	25-44	Summer

AI Model Prediction Output:

The AI model predicts the success of future campaigns based on the past data, particularly focusing on Ad Spend, Conversion Rate, and Time of Year.

Predicted Campaign ID	Predicted Revenue ($)	Predicted Conversion Rate (%)	Predicted ROI (%)	Ad Spend ($)	Time of Year
6	3500	12.0	250%	700	Winter
7	2000	10.5	200%	500	Fall

Output and Results:

1. **Predicted Revenue and Conversion Rates**: For the upcoming campaigns (6 and 7), the model predicts a revenue of $3500 and $2000, respectively. This prediction is based on factors like ad spend and the success of similar campaigns in the past.

2. **ROI Predictions**: The model predicts a return on investment (ROI) of 250% for Campaign 6, meaning for every dollar spent, the company expects to earn $2.50. Campaign 7 has a lower ROI prediction at 200%, which is still profitable but less than Campaign 6.

3. **Campaign Timing**: Campaign 6, which is scheduled for the winter, is predicted to perform better than Campaign 7, which will take place in the fall. This indicates that historical data shows winter campaigns tend to yield higher returns, possibly due to seasonal shopping behavior.

Interpretation of Results and Observations:

- **Higher Revenue with Higher Ad Spend**: Campaign 6's higher ad spend correlates with a higher predicted revenue. This suggests that investing more in certain periods (winter) yields better results.

- **Time of Year Impact**: Winter campaigns appear to have better results compared to fall ones. The AI model considers historical patterns, including seasonal consumer behavior, in its predictions.

- **Targeting and Budgeting Decisions**: With the prediction of a higher ROI for Campaign 6, the marketing team might consider increasing the budget for this campaign, particularly since it falls during a more profitable season.

- **Conversion Rate Optimization**: While the conversion rates are lower for Campaign 7, it still generates a solid ROI. The team may focus on improving conversion rates through optimized ad copy, better targeting, or improved website features.

E-Commerce Perspective Decisions:

1. **Budget Allocation**: Increase the budget for Campaign 6 as it is predicted to generate a higher ROI and revenue, capitalizing on the winter shopping period.

2. **Refining Targeting**: Focus on refining the targeting strategy for Campaign 7 to boost its conversion rate and make it more competitive with Campaign 6 in terms of revenue.

3. **Seasonal Strategy**: Utilize the AI model's insight on seasonal trends to plan future campaigns around the periods with historically higher conversion rates (winter over fall, in this case).

Overall, AI-driven predictions help the company make more informed decisions, leading to optimized marketing strategies and better resource allocation.

12. The Future of Generative AI and AI in E-Commerce

Generative AI has the potential to revolutionize e-commerce by enabling more personalized and engaging shopping experiences. Through the use of advanced algorithms, AI can generate customized product recommendations based on individual customer preferences, browsing behavior, and purchase history. This ability to predict what a customer is likely to be interested in allows e-commerce platforms to offer a highly tailored shopping experience, increasing the likelihood of conversion and customer satisfaction.

AI is also enhancing the way businesses manage inventory and supply chains. Predictive algorithms can help companies anticipate demand, optimize stock levels, and even forecast future trends in consumer behavior.

This not only reduces waste but ensures that popular products are readily available when customers want them. In turn, businesses can improve their operational efficiency and reduce costs, leading to better profitability and customer service.

The role of generative AI in content creation for e-commerce is another game-changer. AI can automatically generate product descriptions, social media posts, and marketing materials that are not only relevant but engaging. By understanding the language and tone that resonates with different customer segments, AI-driven tools can create content at scale, allowing businesses to maintain a consistent brand voice across multiple platforms without overwhelming human teams. This opens up new opportunities for marketers to focus on strategy rather than repetitive tasks.

AI-powered chatbots and virtual assistants are becoming increasingly common in customer service. These tools can engage customers in real-time, answer questions, resolve issues, and even guide them through the purchasing process. As AI continues to improve, these chatbots will become more sophisticated, offering increasingly human-like interactions that create a seamless and satisfying shopping experience. Customers will appreciate having their needs met quickly, without the frustration of waiting for human support.

In terms of personalization, generative AI is helping to move beyond basic recommendations. It can now create entire shopping experiences for individual users by curating a selection of products that fit their specific tastes, budget, and even the occasion. By analyzing not just the purchase history but also contextual factors like the user's location, season, or lifestyle preferences, AI can present shoppers with a dynamic set of options that feels unique to them, making their shopping journey feel more special.

Looking ahead, the integration of augmented reality (AR) and virtual reality (VR) with AI could further enhance the e-commerce experience. Generative AI could generate realistic 3D models of products that customers can interact with virtually, helping them make more informed decisions before purchasing. This fusion of technologies promises to break down the barriers of online shopping, making it feel as though consumers are physically engaging with products in a store. As this technology matures, it will likely become a significant factor in driving the future of e-commerce, creating new opportunities for both businesses and consumers.

Practical Example: The Future of Generative AI and AI in E-Commerce

Generative AI is revolutionizing the e-commerce sector by enhancing personalization, streamlining operations, and improving customer experience. In a practical scenario, an e-commerce company uses generative AI tools to analyze customer behavior, generate product recommendations, create personalized marketing content, and optimize inventory management. The company also utilizes AI-powered chatbots and virtual assistants to provide 24/7 customer service. By integrating AI, the company can optimize sales, reduce costs, and enhance customer engagement. Below is an example of how generative AI can impact the sales of a fictional e-commerce store by analyzing customer interaction and purchases over a month.

Sample Data: E-Commerce Sales Analysis

Customer Segment	Pre-AI Sales (USD)	AI-Optimized Sales (USD)	Increase in Sales (%)	AI-Generated Recommendations	Conversion Rate Improvement (%)
New Customers	50,000	75,000	50%	Personalized product suggestions	20%
Returning Customers	80,000	112,000	40%	Targeted email campaigns	18%
High-Value Customers	100,000	150,000	50%	Personalized offers and discounts	25%
Casual Shoppers	30,000	45,000	50%	Dynamic pricing and bundles	30%

Output and Results:

1. **Increase in Sales**: Generative AI has helped each customer segment increase sales by 40-50%. For example, sales from new customers increased from $50,000 to $75,000, showing a 50% boost.

2. **AI-Generated Recommendations**: AI-driven personalized product suggestions have significantly contributed to sales growth. These tailored recommendations were a key factor in improving conversion rates.

3. **Conversion Rate Improvement**: AI has improved the conversion rate across all segments, especially for casual shoppers (30%) and high-value customers (25%).

Observations:

- **Impact on Sales**: Generative AI improved sales across all customer segments, with high-value customers showing the most significant increase in sales. This suggests that personalized offers for high-value customers yield higher returns.

- **Conversion Rate**: AI's ability to tailor recommendations and create dynamic pricing models resulted in significant improvements in conversion rates, especially among casual shoppers. This demonstrates that AI can effectively convert low-engagement visitors into buyers.

- **Cost Efficiency**: By automating personalized marketing campaigns and inventory management, AI reduces the need for manual intervention, saving both time and operational costs.

Decisions from the E-Commerce Perspective:

1. **Invest in AI for Personalization**: E-commerce businesses should prioritize AI tools that generate personalized content and recommendations. Targeting customers with tailored products and offers can lead to increased sales and higher conversion rates.

2. **Focus on High-Value Customers**: AI's ability to personalize offers for high-value customers should be a core strategy, as it delivers the highest returns in terms of revenue increase.

3. **Utilize AI for Dynamic Pricing**: Incorporating dynamic pricing and bundles can be particularly beneficial for casual shoppers, driving conversions and increasing total sales.

4. **Scale AI Across All Segments**: While AI showed the most impact with high-value customers, scaling AI-driven strategies to all customer segments will lead to sustained growth and more efficient resource allocation.

In conclusion, the future of generative AI in e-commerce is promising, offering enhanced sales, better customer engagement, and more efficient operations.

12.1 Trends in AI-Driven E-Commerce

AI-driven e-commerce has significantly transformed the shopping experience in recent years, helping businesses personalize offerings and improve customer service. One of the most prominent trends is the rise of personalized shopping experiences. By analyzing customer data, AI algorithms can predict user preferences and offer tailored recommendations based on browsing history, purchasing habits, and demographic information. This level of customization not only increases customer satisfaction but also drives higher conversion rates by showing customers products they are more likely to purchase.

Another growing trend is the use of AI chatbots and virtual assistants. These tools are capable of handling a variety of customer service functions, such as answering questions, guiding users through the buying process, and resolving issues in real-time. With natural language processing and machine learning, these chatbots have become more sophisticated, providing a seamless and efficient interaction that mimics human-like conversation. This reduces the need for human customer support and ensures that customers can get immediate assistance at any time of day.

AI is also playing a critical role in improving inventory management and supply chain operations. By analyzing vast amounts of data, AI can predict demand trends and optimize stock levels. This enables businesses to reduce the risk of overstocking or running out of popular items, leading to a more efficient inventory system and reducing costs. AI's ability to forecast trends in consumer behavior helps e-commerce companies better plan for seasonal changes, promotional events, and shifts in customer preferences.

Furthermore, AI has become an integral tool for dynamic pricing strategies. Through the analysis of competitor pricing, market demand, and consumer behavior, AI-powered systems can automatically adjust prices in real time to maximize profitability. This flexible approach allows e-commerce businesses to stay competitive in fast-paced markets while ensuring they can offer the best prices for their customers. AI-driven dynamic pricing can also help businesses respond quickly to shifts in the market, making their pricing strategies more agile.

AI's ability to enhance visual search capabilities is another key trend in e-commerce. Customers can now upload images of products they are interested in, and AI algorithms can identify similar items available for purchase. This functionality removes the need for traditional text-based searches, allowing shoppers to find products faster and more accurately. Visual search technology is especially popular in fashion and home décor, where finding similar items based on visual appearance is crucial for customers.

Lastly, the role of AI in fraud detection and security cannot be overstated. With the increasing number of online transactions, AI systems are being employed to monitor and analyze patterns of customer behavior to detect fraudulent activities. These systems can identify unusual transaction patterns, flag potential security threats, and take proactive measures to prevent fraud. This not only protects businesses from financial loss but also builds trust with customers who feel their personal and financial data is secure.

Practical Example: Exploring the Future Role of AI and Automation in E-Commerce Personalization

E-commerce businesses are increasingly turning to AI and automation to enhance personalized shopping experiences, with the goal of increasing customer satisfaction, loyalty, and conversion rates. AI tools analyze customer behavior, preferences, and previous interactions to provide tailored recommendations and dynamic pricing, which can be more effective than traditional marketing techniques. For instance, an e-commerce platform uses AI-driven recommendation engines that suggest products based on past purchases and browsing history. This type of personalization helps customers discover products they are likely to buy, improving the likelihood of conversions and boosting overall sales.

Sample Data: Increasing Use of AI for Personalized Experiences in E-Commerce

Year	AI Integration in Personalization (%)	Conversion Rate (%)	Average Order Value ($)	Customer Retention Rate (%)
2020	30	5	45	60
2021	50	8	55	65
2022	70	12	70	70
2023	85	15	85	75
2024	95	18	100	80

Output and Results:

- **AI Integration in Personalization**: The percentage of e-commerce platforms integrating AI for personalization has increased significantly from 30% in 2020 to 95% in 2024.

- **Conversion Rate**: As AI integration grows, the conversion rate increases from 5% in 2020 to 18% in 2024.

- **Average Order Value (AOV)**: The average order value rises from $45 in 2020 to $100 in 2024.

- **Customer Retention Rate**: Retention rates have also steadily improved, reaching 80% in 2024.

Explanation and Interpretation:

1. **Increasing AI Integration**: The rise in AI integration suggests that more e-commerce businesses are leveraging automation and personalized recommendations, which makes shopping experiences more relevant to individual customers.

2. **Improved Conversion Rates**: With higher AI adoption, personalized experiences are driving better customer engagement and higher conversion rates. Tailored suggestions make it easier for customers to find and purchase items they are interested in, which explains the growing conversion rate.

3. **Increased Average Order Value**: Personalized experiences often lead to upselling and cross-selling opportunities, resulting in higher average order values. For example, a recommendation engine might suggest accessories or related products, prompting customers to make larger purchases.

4. **Higher Customer Retention**: As personalization improves, customers are more likely to return to a platform they feel understands their preferences, leading to higher retention rates.

Observations:

- The trend toward AI-powered personalization is having a clear and positive impact on key metrics such as conversion rates, average order values, and customer retention.

- E-commerce businesses that implement AI and automation effectively are likely to see better financial performance and customer loyalty.

- As AI capabilities continue to improve, there may be further optimization opportunities, such as real-time personalization or predictive analytics to anticipate customer needs even before they realize them.

Decisions from the E-Commerce Perspective:

1. **Invest in AI Tools**: E-commerce businesses should continue investing in AI and machine learning technologies to further enhance personalization and stay competitive.

2. **Focus on Customer Experience**: Businesses must prioritize creating seamless and intuitive personalized shopping journeys, using data to anticipate customer needs and increase satisfaction.

3. **Leverage Data**: Utilize customer data to refine recommendation algorithms and create more targeted marketing campaigns, which will help increase conversion rates and boost customer loyalty.

4. **Monitor Metrics Regularly**: Track the key performance indicators (KPIs) like conversion rates, order values, and retention rates to evaluate the success of AI-driven personalization strategies and make adjustments as needed.

12.2 Ethical Considerations in AI for E-Commerce

Ethical considerations in AI for e-commerce are crucial as technology continues to shape the industry. One of the main ethical concerns revolves around consumer privacy. With the vast amounts of data AI systems can collect, it is essential to ensure that personal information is protected and used responsibly. E-commerce platforms must be transparent about data collection practices and allow consumers to have control over their information, avoiding misuse and unauthorized sharing with third parties.

Another challenge is ensuring fairness in AI algorithms. AI systems are often trained on large datasets, which can inadvertently reflect biases present in society. These biases can lead to unfair outcomes, such as discrimination against certain groups of consumers based on factors like race, gender, or socioeconomic status. E-commerce companies must strive to create AI systems that are designed to be unbiased, taking proactive steps to ensure fairness in product recommendations, pricing, and advertisements.

AI also raises concerns about transparency in decision-making. Consumers often interact with AI-driven systems without understanding how decisions are made. This lack of transparency can make it difficult for customers to trust the system, especially if they feel they are being manipulated or misled. To address this, companies should aim for greater transparency by explaining how their AI models work, including what data is used and how it influences decisions, giving consumers more confidence in their interactions with AI-powered systems.

Moreover, the implementation of AI in e-commerce has the potential to impact employment. As AI systems automate more processes, such as inventory management, customer service, and personalized marketing, human jobs may be replaced or diminished. While AI can lead to increased efficiency and cost savings, it is important to consider the social implications. Companies should look for ways to balance the use of AI with the well-being of their workforce, ensuring that displaced workers have opportunities for retraining and new roles.

The environmental impact of AI is another consideration in e-commerce. AI requires significant computational power, which in turn demands energy consumption and contributes to carbon emissions. As e-commerce businesses scale their use of AI, they should prioritize sustainability by exploring ways to reduce the energy consumption of their AI models and investing in green technologies. This will help mitigate the negative environmental effects of widespread AI adoption.

Lastly, consumer manipulation is a growing concern with AI in e-commerce. Personalized recommendations and targeted advertisements, while effective for driving sales, can also be used in ways that manipulate consumer behavior, often exploiting psychological vulnerabilities. Companies should be mindful of ethical boundaries when designing AI systems that interact with consumers, ensuring that these systems respect user autonomy and do not encourage unhealthy or exploitative consumption patterns. Balancing business goals with consumer well-being is essential to maintaining trust and loyalty in the long term.

Practical Example Context:

In an e-commerce platform, an AI recommendation system suggests products to users based on their browsing history, demographics, and previous purchases. However, biases in the algorithm can arise, such as favoring certain product categories or brands that align with the platform's partnerships or user behavior trends. This can lead to unequal representation or unfair recommendations for specific groups of customers, such as gender or age-related biases. Addressing this bias and ensuring transparency is crucial for ethical AI deployment. The example below showcases how AI-generated recommendations might reflect bias, and how transparency can help improve fairness.

Sample Data: AI-Generated Recommendations with Ethical Implications

Customer ID	Gender	Age Group	Browsing History	Recommended Products	Ethical Implications
001	Female	25-34	Shoes, Dresses	Heels, Skirts, Handbags	Overrepresentation of fashion; ignores tech products
002	Male	18-24	Electronics, Games	Laptops, Gaming Consoles, Headphones	Gender bias towards electronics and games
003	Female	45-54	Home Decor, Books	Cozy Chairs, Wall Art, Cookware	Stereotypical assumptions

Customer ID	Gender	Age Group	Browsing History	Recommended Products	Ethical Implications
					about women's interests
004	Male	35-44	Sports, Fitness	Running Shoes, Dumbbells, Water Bottles	Gender bias towards physical activity
005	Female	55-64	Health, Kitchen Appliances	Blenders, Cookware, Supplements	Age and gender bias favoring domestic products

Output and Results:

1. **Bias in Recommendations:**

   o **Gender Bias:** The recommendations for males predominantly feature electronics and sports-related products, while females are mostly shown fashion and home-related items.

   o **Age Bias:** Younger customers are recommended electronics or gaming products, while older customers receive recommendations focused on home decor, health, or kitchen appliances.

2. **Transparency Implications:**

   o The recommendations lack transparency about how they are tailored to each customer's preferences or how algorithms are designed. This might alienate users who feel their preferences are not being understood or respected.

Interpretation of Results and Output:

The AI recommendations show clear biases based on both gender and age group. For example, the system overemphasizes traditionally gendered products—tech and games for men, fashion and home decor for women. Moreover, older age groups are typically recommended products for health or home use, further entrenching stereotypes about interests linked to age.

The lack of diversity in these recommendations can lead to user dissatisfaction, poor user experience, and even ethical concerns.

Observations:

- There is a need to diversify AI models to account for different preferences and remove the influence of gender or age stereotypes.
- The recommendations could also consider broader user data, such as preferences for varied product categories, rather than narrow, demographic-driven suggestions.
- Ethical implications could result in alienating specific user groups, reducing trust in the platform.

Decisions from the E-Commerce Perspective:

1. **Improve Diversity in Recommendations:**
   - Update the AI model to include a wider variety of interests across gender and age demographics.
   - Use more transparent algorithms that explain why certain products are recommended, allowing users to see the rationale behind suggestions.

2. **Bias Mitigation Strategies:**
   - Apply fairness constraints during model training to ensure equal representation of product categories for all demographics.
   - Introduce mechanisms where the system cross-references users' past behavior with their current preferences to avoid stereotyping.

3. **Transparency and User Control:**
   - Provide users with an option to refine or adjust their preferences for recommendations (e.g., by genre, price, or style).
   - Offer a transparency report or dashboard showing how recommendations are generated, ensuring users understand the underlying AI model.

By addressing these issues, e-commerce platforms can improve user satisfaction, build trust, and foster a more inclusive and ethical AI recommendation system.

12.3 The Impact of AI and Automation on E-Commerce Workforce

The rise of AI and automation is having a significant impact on the e-commerce workforce. As businesses integrate advanced technologies like machine learning, robotic process automation, and artificial intelligence into their operations, many manual and repetitive tasks are being automated. This has led to a reduction in the demand for traditional roles that previously handled customer service inquiries, inventory management, and order processing. These roles are being replaced by algorithms that can efficiently manage vast amounts of data and perform tasks with greater speed and accuracy than humans.

Despite the reduction in certain jobs, AI and automation have also created new opportunities in the e-commerce industry. As technology advances, there is an increasing demand for workers skilled in programming, data analysis, and AI development. The implementation of automation also opens doors for roles in the maintenance and supervision of automated systems. The workforce is being reshaped, with a greater emphasis on technical expertise to manage, design, and improve the systems that power e-commerce operations.

AI is also revolutionizing customer experience, which impacts the workforce in different ways. Chatbots and virtual assistants are becoming more sophisticated, able to handle customer inquiries around the clock without human intervention. This reduces the need for large customer service teams, but it also demands a different skill set from employees who focus on more complex issues or areas where AI cannot provide a solution. Workers need to adapt and focus on tasks that require human creativity, empathy, and decision-making that machines cannot replicate.

Moreover, the use of automation in warehouses and fulfillment centers has transformed the logistics side of e-commerce. Automated robots can sort, pick, and pack products at speeds far exceeding human workers. While this reduces the number of jobs in warehouses, it also creates a need for new roles in overseeing robotic operations and ensuring the systems run smoothly. The workforce in this area must now be equipped with the knowledge to handle these advanced machines and manage the technology that supports them.

AI-driven analytics and data management have altered the way e-commerce companies understand and cater to their customers. With the ability to analyze vast amounts of data, businesses can offer personalized recommendations and targeted marketing strategies. This shift requires a workforce that is capable of interpreting data and utilizing insights to improve product offerings, marketing campaigns, and customer engagement. Data-driven decision-making is now a key skill for employees in e-commerce, which means many workers need to upskill to remain competitive in the market.

In conclusion, while AI and automation are disrupting traditional jobs within the e-commerce workforce, they are also paving the way for the creation of new positions and skill sets. The workforce must adapt to these changes by acquiring new technical knowledge and focusing on tasks that complement automation, such as creative problem-solving, managing AI systems, and improving customer relationships in ways machines cannot. This shift offers opportunities for workers who are willing to embrace the future of technology and continue developing the skills required for the next generation of e-commerce jobs.

Practical Example: AI and Automation Transforming Customer Service Jobs in E-Commerce

In an e-commerce company, AI-driven chatbots have been integrated into the customer support system to handle routine inquiries, improve response times, and reduce the workload on human agents. The AI chatbot is programmed to address common queries such as order tracking, product information, and return policies. The company tracks the efficiency of the chatbot in resolving customer queries versus human agents over a one-month period. The objective is to assess the impact on customer satisfaction, response time, and the number of cases handled by human agents.

Sample Data (Before and After AI Chatbot Integration)

Metric	Before AI Chatbot	After AI Chatbot	% Change
Average Response Time (min)	5.2	1.1	-78.8%
Human Agent Involvement	60%	25%	-58.3%
Customer Satisfaction Score	85%	90%	+5.9%

Metric	Before AI Chatbot	After AI Chatbot	% Change
Total Queries Handled (per day)	200	350	+75%
Resolution Time for Issues	8.5 min	3.2 min	-62.4%
Employee Overtime Hours	80 hours/month	40 hours/month	-50%

Explanation and Interpretation of Results:

- **Average Response Time:** The introduction of the AI chatbot significantly decreased the average response time from 5.2 minutes to 1.1 minutes, representing a reduction of 78.8%. This indicates that customers are receiving quicker responses to their inquiries, improving their overall experience.

- **Human Agent Involvement:** The percentage of queries requiring human intervention dropped from 60% to 25%. This shows that AI is efficiently handling a large portion of the routine and simple queries, freeing human agents to focus on more complex issues.

- **Customer Satisfaction Score:** Customer satisfaction increased from 85% to 90%, a 5.9% improvement. This suggests that faster response times and more accurate answers provided by the AI chatbot have contributed to higher levels of customer satisfaction.

- **Total Queries Handled:** The chatbot's efficiency led to a 75% increase in the number of queries handled per day. This is due to the chatbot's ability to address multiple queries simultaneously, which human agents cannot do.

- **Resolution Time for Issues:** The time to resolve customer issues decreased by 62.4%, from 8.5 minutes to 3.2 minutes. AI chatbots help resolve issues quickly by providing automated solutions to common problems, speeding up the resolution process.

- **Employee Overtime Hours:** The reduction in employee overtime hours by 50% reflects the decreased workload of human agents. They are now more focused on handling complex or escalated issues, while the chatbot deals with simpler cases.

Observations:

- **Increased Efficiency:** AI has drastically improved operational efficiency, reducing human agents' workload and improving the speed of response times.

- **Higher Customer Satisfaction:** The faster, more accurate responses from the chatbot seem to have had a positive impact on customer satisfaction, as evidenced by the 5.9% increase in the satisfaction score.

- **Cost Reduction:** Fewer overtime hours and less reliance on human agents for basic queries could reduce labor costs, enabling the company to allocate resources to more strategic areas.

Decisions from the E-Commerce Perspective:

1. **Expand AI Chatbot Usage:** Given the positive impact on customer service efficiency and customer satisfaction, the e-commerce company should consider expanding the chatbot's capabilities to handle more complex queries. This would further reduce human agent workload and increase efficiency.

2. **Invest in AI Training:** Continuous improvements in chatbot capabilities through machine learning and natural language processing (NLP) can help improve the chatbot's ability to handle a broader range of queries, ultimately decreasing human agent dependency even further.

3. **Enhance Human Agent Roles:** With routine tasks being handled by AI, the company can shift the focus of human agents toward more complex customer issues or higher-value tasks like product recommendations or personalized service.

4. **Monitor Customer Feedback:** While customer satisfaction has improved, it's essential to continuously monitor feedback to ensure the AI does not compromise the quality of service, particularly for more nuanced issues.

In conclusion, the integration of AI and automation in e-commerce customer service has proven to be a game-changer in terms of efficiency, cost savings, and customer satisfaction.

13. Real-world case study examples

13.1 Case Study 1: AI-Powered Personalized Marketing in E-Commerce – Amazon

Company Overview:

Amazon, one of the largest and most influential e-commerce platforms globally, has pioneered the integration of AI into its business strategy to drive personalized marketing and improve customer experiences. With over 300 million active customer accounts, Amazon leverages AI to deliver tailored shopping experiences, optimize marketing efforts, and enhance customer engagement.

2. Personalized Marketing with AI in E-Commerce

Amazon's use of artificial intelligence to deliver personalized marketing is a prime example of how e-commerce platforms can enhance customer satisfaction and boost sales. The company employs AI in various aspects, including customer segmentation, product recommendations, and dynamic pricing.

2.1 AI-Driven Customer Segmentation in E-Commerce

Amazon utilizes AI algorithms to segment its vast customer base into different groups based on purchase behavior, preferences, and browsing history. The segmentation helps Amazon create targeted marketing campaigns, offering relevant products and promotions. By grouping customers into personalized segments, Amazon increases the chances of converting potential buyers.

For instance, Amazon's AI-driven recommendation engine processes past purchase history, search queries, and browsing patterns to create detailed customer profiles. This segmentation enables Amazon to send tailored email newsletters and ads to each customer group, significantly enhancing the likelihood of conversions.

2.2 Product Recommendations Using Collaborative Filtering in E-Commerce

One of the key innovations Amazon uses to personalize its e-commerce experience is **collaborative filtering**. This AI technique analyzes user behavior—like clicks, purchases, and ratings—to predict products a customer might like. Collaborative filtering works by identifying similarities between users and recommending products based on what other users with similar behaviors have liked.

For example, if a customer buys a book about machine learning, Amazon will recommend other books in the same genre or related topics, even if the user hasn't directly shown interest in those particular books. This type of personalized recommendation system has been a driving force behind Amazon's "Customers who bought this also bought" and "Frequently bought together" features, contributing to increased sales and higher average order values.

2.3 Dynamic Pricing with AI in E-Commerce

Dynamic pricing is another area where Amazon applies AI to personalize the shopping experience. By continuously analyzing market conditions, competitor pricing, demand fluctuations, and customer behavior, Amazon adjusts the prices of its products in real-time.

The use of AI allows Amazon to implement personalized pricing strategies, offering specific discounts or price changes to individual customers based on factors such as their browsing habits, location, or membership in programs like Amazon Prime. This flexible pricing model enhances customer satisfaction by providing a tailored shopping experience while maximizing revenue for Amazon.

Challenges in Implementing AI in E-Commerce:

Despite its success, Amazon has encountered several challenges in implementing AI-driven personalized marketing strategies:

1. **Data Privacy Concerns:** The more Amazon personalizes its offerings, the more customer data it collects. While AI thrives on large datasets, managing this data ethically and ensuring customer privacy is a constant challenge. Amazon has had to invest in advanced security systems to protect sensitive customer information and comply with global data protection regulations such as GDPR.

2. **Balancing Automation and Human Touch:** AI recommendations and marketing automation can sometimes feel impersonal, making it essential for Amazon to maintain a balance between AI-driven marketing and human interaction. Ensuring that customers don't

feel overwhelmed by too many automated suggestions or ads requires careful tuning of algorithms.

3. **Integration Across Multiple Platforms:** Amazon's AI marketing strategies must be seamlessly integrated across different platforms, including its website, mobile app, and third-party services like Alexa. The complexity of ensuring consistent personalized marketing across all touchpoints requires advanced AI systems and cross-platform integration.

Conclusion:

Amazon's AI-driven personalized marketing is a prime example of how e-commerce companies can leverage artificial intelligence to enhance customer engagement, improve sales, and create highly tailored shopping experiences. While challenges such as data privacy and balancing automation with human interaction persist, Amazon continues to push the boundaries of what is possible with AI in the e-commerce space.

13.2 Case Study 2: AI in E-Commerce at Walmart

Company Overview:

Walmart, one of the largest global retail chains, has been an early adopter of artificial intelligence (AI) across its e-commerce operations. The company uses AI to streamline inventory management, enhance customer experience, and optimize its pricing strategies. Walmart has integrated various AI technologies into its business models, driving growth in its online sales and improving operational efficiency.

Case Study: AI-Powered Customer Experience and Personalization at Walmart

---

1. AI in E-Commerce:

1.1 Role of AI in E-Commerce:

AI has become a cornerstone of Walmart's e-commerce strategy. The company uses AI to power several key areas of its operations, including:

- **Personalized Customer Experience:** AI helps Walmart offer highly personalized experiences for shoppers by analyzing their purchasing behavior, location, and preferences. This data-driven approach allows Walmart to recommend products tailored to individual customers.

- **Dynamic Pricing:** Walmart employs AI to set competitive and dynamic prices based on factors like demand, supply, competitor pricing, and seasonality. This enables Walmart to adjust its prices in real-time and stay ahead of competitors in the fast-paced retail environment.

- **Inventory Management:** AI is used to predict product demand and optimize inventory levels. Walmart applies AI algorithms to forecast demand patterns, ensuring that products are available when customers need them while minimizing overstock.

1.2 Challenges in Implementing AI in E-Commerce:

- **Data Integration and Quality:** One of the biggest challenges Walmart faces is integrating vast amounts of data from different sources, including customer data, inventory data, and transaction history. Ensuring that this data is clean, accurate, and usable for AI models is a constant hurdle.

- **Scalability of AI Systems:** Walmart operates globally, so scaling AI solutions across different regions and product categories presents challenges. The infrastructure needs to support large-scale AI applications without compromising performance.

- **Cost of Implementation:** Developing, training, and deploying AI models at scale is a costly process. Walmart must carefully balance the cost of AI technology with the potential return on investment, ensuring that AI-driven initiatives lead to significant operational efficiency and customer satisfaction gains.

1.3 Data Management Strategies for E-Commerce:

To manage the large volumes of data generated through e-commerce, Walmart employs the following strategies:

- **Centralized Data Warehousing:** Walmart collects data from various sources into a centralized repository where it can be easily accessed, analyzed, and used for AI-driven insights. This centralized approach ensures that the data is consistent and accessible across all departments.

- **Advanced Analytics:** Walmart uses AI and machine learning algorithms to analyze the data for insights into customer behavior, product trends, and operational performance. This helps the company optimize everything from marketing strategies to supply chain logistics.

- **Data Quality Control:** Walmart has invested in robust data cleaning and validation processes to ensure that the data fed into its AI systems is of high quality, which is critical for the success of any AI-powered applications.

1.4 Data Privacy and Security Concerns in E-Commerce:

Walmart handles vast amounts of personal and transaction data from millions of customers. To ensure data privacy and security:

- **Compliance with Regulations:** Walmart adheres to global data privacy regulations like the GDPR in the European Union and CCPA in California. It ensures that customer data is handled in a compliant and secure manner.

- **Encryption and Secure Storage:** Walmart employs advanced encryption technologies to protect customer data both at rest and in transit. This helps prevent unauthorized access to sensitive information.

- **Transparency and Customer Consent:** Walmart maintains transparency about how customer data is collected and used. Customers are informed about their data rights and can opt out of data collection practices, ensuring trust and compliance with privacy regulations.

2. AI-Driven Customer Segmentation and Product Recommendations

2.1 AI-Driven Customer Segmentation in E-Commerce:

Walmart uses AI to segment its vast customer base into different groups based on purchasing behavior, demographics, and browsing history. These segments enable Walmart to target specific customer groups with personalized product offerings and tailored marketing messages.

For instance, Walmart might target high-frequency shoppers with exclusive promotions or offer first-time shoppers recommendations based on what similar customers have purchased. This segmentation helps Walmart increase conversion rates and drive repeat business.

2.2 Product Recommendations Using Collaborative Filtering in E-Commerce:

Walmart's recommendation engine uses collaborative filtering, a popular AI technique, to suggest products based on the preferences of similar customers. For example, if a customer purchases a pair of running shoes, the system might recommend related products such as athletic apparel or accessories that other customers bought alongside the shoes.

Collaborative filtering helps Walmart drive cross-selling and upselling opportunities, boosting average order values and improving customer satisfaction by showcasing products the customer is likely to find relevant.

2.3 Dynamic Pricing with AI in E-Commerce:

Walmart uses AI-powered dynamic pricing to ensure that its prices remain competitive and maximize profitability. The AI system analyzes a range of factors, including market trends, competitor pricing, inventory levels, and demand forecasts, to adjust prices in real time.

For example, if a product is in high demand during the holiday season, the system might raise the price slightly to capitalize on the demand. Conversely, if a product is overstocked or nearing its expiration date, the price may be lowered to encourage sales.

3. Building AI-Powered Chatbots for Customer Support

3.1 Data Cleaning and Transformation in E-Commerce:

Walmart's chatbot solutions require significant data cleaning and transformation to ensure that the data used for customer interactions is accurate and up-to-date. AI models rely on clean, structured data to respond to customer queries effectively and offer personalized solutions.

3.2 Enhancing Customer Experience with Virtual Shopping Assistants:

Walmart's virtual shopping assistants, powered by AI, enhance the customer experience by guiding users through the shopping journey. The AI assistant can help customers find products, check product availability, track orders, and even offer personalized recommendations based on previous purchases and browsing behavior.

This AI-driven assistant mimics a human-like conversation, making the shopping experience more seamless and interactive. It also reduces the burden on human customer service agents by handling repetitive tasks and common queries.

3.3 Natural Language Processing (NLP) for Customer Interaction:

Walmart uses NLP to power its chatbots, allowing them to understand and respond to customer inquiries in natural language. NLP enables Walmart's AI to process and interpret a wide range of customer queries, from product questions to shipping status updates.

This makes interactions more intuitive for customers, as they can communicate with the AI assistant using everyday language. Over time, the system continues to learn from these interactions, improving its accuracy and effectiveness.

Conclusion:

Walmart's integration of AI in its e-commerce strategy has enabled the company to deliver highly personalized shopping experiences, optimize inventory management, and maintain competitive pricing. Despite challenges such as data integration, privacy concerns, and the cost of AI implementation, Walmart continues to invest in AI to streamline operations, enhance customer satisfaction, and drive sales growth. The company's use of AI-powered product recommendations, dynamic pricing, and virtual shopping assistants has set a new standard in e-commerce innovation, providing valuable insights for other retailers looking to adopt similar technologies.

13.3 Case Study 3: AI in E-Commerce – Product Recommendations Using Collaborative Filtering (AI-Driven Customer Experience) at Amazon

AI is a key enabler in modern e-commerce platforms, helping businesses deliver highly personalized and optimized shopping experiences for customers. Amazon, the largest e-commerce company globally, uses AI to provide users with product recommendations that are based on individual preferences and purchasing behaviors. Collaborative filtering, a key technique in machine learning, is central to this process. It allows Amazon to predict products that users are likely to buy by analyzing patterns of behavior from other similar customers. This enhances the overall shopping experience and drives sales.

1.2 Challenges in Implementing AI in E-Commerce:

Despite its effectiveness, implementing AI in e-commerce comes with several challenges:

- **Data Privacy and Security:** Collecting and analyzing vast amounts of consumer data, including past purchases, browsing history, and personal preferences, requires strict data privacy and security measures. Any breach could harm Amazon's reputation and lead to legal consequences.

- **Data Quality:** AI models, such as collaborative filtering, are only as good as the data they are trained on. Amazon needs high-quality data that is both diverse and accurate to ensure the recommendations are reliable and relevant.

- **Scalability:** With millions of products and users, scaling AI algorithms to provide personalized experiences to each customer in real time is a significant challenge. Amazon needs highly optimized infrastructure and algorithms to handle this scale.

1.3 Data Management Strategies for E-Commerce:

Amazon uses advanced data management strategies to handle vast amounts of data efficiently:

- **Data Lakes and Cloud Computing:** Amazon stores its data in scalable cloud infrastructure, which allows it to manage, process, and analyze massive amounts of structured and unstructured data.

Amazon Web Services (AWS) plays a key role in this, ensuring that the company can handle large-scale AI-driven recommendations seamlessly.

- **Real-Time Data Processing:** For collaborative filtering to work in real-time, Amazon needs to continuously update its data on customer behavior, interactions, and transactions. Real-time data processing frameworks, like Apache Kafka and AWS Lambda, help Amazon deliver instant and relevant product recommendations to users.

1.4 Data Privacy and Security Concerns in E-Commerce:

Handling personal data is a significant responsibility. Amazon must comply with privacy laws such as the GDPR in Europe and other regional regulations. To ensure security and privacy, Amazon has implemented:

- **Data Anonymization:** Amazon anonymizes customer data to prevent personal information from being directly linked to individual users, protecting customer privacy.

- **Encryption:** All sensitive customer information, including payment details and address information, is encrypted both during transit and at rest to protect it from cyber threats.

- **User Consent:** Amazon allows users to manage their preferences and opt-in to data collection, ensuring compliance with global privacy standards.

Case Application: Product Recommendations Using Collaborative Filtering:

- **How It Works:** Collaborative filtering works by analyzing historical data across users. When a customer browses Amazon's website or makes a purchase, Amazon's AI algorithms compare their behavior to that of other customers with similar preferences and purchase history. It then recommends products that these similar users have liked or purchased, thereby suggesting items the current customer is likely to be interested in.

- **Example:** If a user frequently buys books on machine learning and AI, the system will suggest other related books, gadgets, or online courses related to this interest. It can also recommend these products to similar users, further refining the algorithm based on user behavior.

- **Results:** This AI-driven product recommendation system has led to significant improvements in conversion rates, increasing the likelihood of additional purchases. According to Amazon, approximately 35% of their revenue is generated by product recommendations alone.

Conclusion:

Amazon's use of collaborative filtering and other AI technologies in its e-commerce operations demonstrates the immense value AI can bring in delivering personalized shopping experiences. While challenges like data privacy, quality, and scalability remain, Amazon's sophisticated data management strategies and strong focus on security have allowed the company to maintain its competitive edge in the e-commerce market. The ability to offer personalized recommendations has not only enhanced customer satisfaction but has also been a key driver in Amazon's continued success.

13.4 Case Study 4: AI-Driven Product Recommendations and Dynamic Pricing in E-Commerce - Amazon

1. Introduction

Amazon, one of the world's largest e-commerce platforms, has effectively leveraged AI to enhance its customer experience and optimize its operations. Two critical aspects of AI in Amazon's business are **product recommendations** and **dynamic pricing**. These AI systems help Amazon maintain a competitive edge, improve customer satisfaction, and increase sales.

2. AI-Driven Product Recommendations Using Collaborative Filtering

2.1 Role of AI in E-Commerce:

Amazon uses AI, specifically **collaborative filtering**, to drive its product recommendation engine. This approach is based on machine learning algorithms that analyze users' past behaviors, such as browsing history, purchase history, and interactions with product reviews, to suggest products that are most likely to appeal to them.

- **Collaborative Filtering**: This technique uses the concept of "users who liked X also liked Y." It creates recommendations by comparing the preferences and behaviors of similar users. For example, if a customer buys a laptop, the system may recommend accessories like laptop bags or external hard drives based on the purchases of other users with similar preferences.

- **Personalization**: Amazon's recommendation engine is personalized to individual users, meaning that no two customers will see the exact same product recommendations. This personalization increases the chances of users purchasing products they find relevant and interesting.

2.2 Challenges in Implementing AI in E-Commerce:

- **Data Overload**: With millions of customers and products, Amazon faces the challenge of handling vast amounts of data. The AI systems must process large datasets to make accurate predictions, and data management becomes critical for successful implementation.

- **Scalability**: As Amazon continues to expand globally, the recommendation algorithms need to be scalable to handle the increasing volume of users and products. Developing AI systems that can scale while maintaining performance is a technical challenge.

- **Diverse User Base**: Amazon's user base spans different regions and demographic groups, each with varying preferences. Ensuring the recommendation system works effectively across this diverse audience while maintaining accuracy is a key challenge.

2.3 Impact on Sales:

The AI-driven product recommendation system is highly successful for Amazon. It has been reported that **35% of Amazon's revenue** comes from its recommendation engine. The system has become an integral part of the platform, providing relevant and timely suggestions that encourage customers to make additional purchases.

3. Dynamic Pricing with AI in E-Commerce

3.1 Role of AI in Dynamic Pricing:

Amazon uses **dynamic pricing** strategies powered by AI to adjust the prices of products in real-time based on factors such as demand, competitor pricing, customer behavior, and market conditions. By continuously analyzing these variables, Amazon ensures that its prices are competitive and optimized for sales.

- **Algorithmic Pricing**: The AI algorithms consider historical data, market trends, competitor prices, and other dynamic factors to adjust the pricing of products automatically. For example, prices for popular electronics may increase during the holiday season when demand is high, while seasonal items may be priced lower to clear out inventory.

- **Competitive Pricing**: Amazon monitors the pricing strategies of its competitors and adjusts its own prices to ensure it remains competitive. AI enables Amazon to make these adjustments rapidly and at scale, ensuring that its prices are always optimized.

3.2 Challenges in Implementing AI for Dynamic Pricing:

- **Market Fluctuations**: In volatile markets, pricing can fluctuate rapidly, and the AI system needs to be able to respond to these changes in real time without causing price discrepancies or frustrating customers.

- **Price Wars**: Dynamic pricing can sometimes lead to aggressive price wars with competitors, which may erode profit margins. Amazon has to balance competitive pricing with the need to maintain profitability.

- **Customer Perception**: Constantly changing prices can lead to customer frustration. Amazon must ensure that price changes do not negatively impact the customer experience, especially if customers feel they are being charged more for the same product over time.

3.3 Benefits of Dynamic Pricing:

- **Revenue Optimization**: Dynamic pricing helps Amazon maximize revenue by adjusting prices in real-time based on market conditions. Products that are in high demand can be priced higher, while slower-moving items can be discounted to stimulate sales.

- **Customer Retention**: By offering competitive prices and deals based on AI insights, Amazon enhances customer satisfaction and increases the likelihood of repeat purchases.

4. Conclusion

Amazon's use of AI-driven product recommendations and dynamic pricing is a testament to how artificial intelligence can be leveraged to create personalized, efficient, and profitable e-commerce strategies. Despite facing challenges like data management, scalability, and competitive pricing, Amazon's AI-driven systems have enabled it to maintain its leadership in the e-commerce space, drive revenue growth, and enhance customer satisfaction.

13.5 Case Study 5: AI-Driven Customer Support with Chatbots - H&M

1. Introduction

H&M, a leading global fashion retailer, has implemented **AI-powered chatbots** for customer support as part of its digital transformation strategy. The company uses AI-driven technology to enhance customer service, reduce response times, and improve the overall shopping experience.

2. Building AI-Powered Chatbots for Customer Support

2.1 Role of AI in E-Commerce:

H&M utilizes AI-powered chatbots to manage and improve customer interactions on its website and mobile app. The primary role of these chatbots is to assist customers with common queries, help navigate the website, and provide personalized product recommendations, all while reducing the need for human agents.

- **Customer Support Automation**: H&M's chatbot handles a variety of customer service inquiries, including order status, product availability, store locations, and shipping information. It is available 24/7, providing customers with quick and accurate responses.

- **Personalized Recommendations**: By using AI, the chatbot can analyze previous interactions and preferences, offering tailored product suggestions based on the customer's browsing history or shopping habits.

2.2 Challenges in Implementing AI in E-Commerce:

- **Natural Language Understanding**: One of the main challenges H&M faces is ensuring that the chatbot can accurately understand and respond to customer queries, especially those with varied language, slang, or informal phrasing. For global companies like H&M, ensuring the AI understands multiple languages and cultural contexts is a complex challenge.

- **Customer Expectations**: Customers have high expectations when it comes to customer service interactions. If the chatbot fails to answer a question correctly or cannot escalate issues to a human agent promptly, it can lead to frustration.

- **Data Privacy and Security**: Since the chatbot collects customer data for personalization, ensuring that this information is securely handled and stored is crucial. Compliance with global data protection regulations, such as GDPR, is a key concern.

2.3 Impact on Customer Service:

Despite these challenges, the implementation of AI-powered chatbots has had a significant positive impact on H&M's customer service. The company has seen improvements in:

- **Reduced Response Time**: The chatbot handles customer queries instantly, reducing wait times and allowing customers to receive help at any time.

- **Cost Efficiency**: By automating repetitive queries, H&M has reduced the need for large human customer service teams, leading to cost savings.

- **Customer Satisfaction**: The availability of 24/7 support and the ability to provide quick, accurate answers has led to improved customer satisfaction. Customers appreciate the convenience and speed of chatbot interactions, especially during off-hours.

3. Data Management Strategies for E-Commerce

3.1 Data Collection and Transformation:

H&M collects data from various sources, including online interactions, purchase history, social media activity, and customer feedback. This data is transformed and processed to feed into the chatbot's AI systems to ensure it delivers relevant and personalized recommendations. The company follows a structured data management approach to ensure that:

- **Data is Clean and Structured**: The data from various channels is cleaned and organized to ensure the AI can interpret it accurately.

- **Real-Time Updates**: The chatbot uses real-time data from H&M's inventory and sales system to provide customers with up-to-date product availability and order status.

3.2 Ensuring Data Security and Compliance:

Since H&M collects personal data from customers, including purchasing behavior and payment details, ensuring that this data is protected from breaches is paramount. The company follows strict data privacy regulations and implements security measures like encryption, regular audits, and secure data storage to ensure customer information is kept safe.

4. Conclusion

H&M's use of AI-powered chatbots for customer support highlights how generative AI and AI-driven solutions can enhance the e-commerce experience. The chatbot offers a fast and scalable solution to handle customer inquiries, provides personalized product recommendations, and ultimately improves customer satisfaction. However, implementing AI in customer service presents challenges such as natural language understanding, data privacy concerns, and customer expectations, all of which H&M has successfully addressed with ongoing improvements to its AI systems.

By leveraging AI for customer support, H&M has positioned itself as a leader in digital transformation within the retail sector, providing efficient, reliable, and personalized services to its global customer base.

13.6 Case Study 6: AI-Driven Dynamic Pricing and Supply Chain Optimization - Zalando

1. Introduction

Zalando, a leading European online fashion and lifestyle retailer, has integrated AI-powered solutions into its pricing and supply chain strategies to enhance customer satisfaction, improve operational efficiency, and increase profitability. The company uses AI-driven **dynamic pricing** models to optimize product prices in real-time, and leverages AI for **inventory replenishment** and **demand forecasting** to streamline its supply chain operations.

2. Dynamic Pricing with AI in E-Commerce

2.1 Role of AI in Dynamic Pricing:

Zalando has developed an AI-based dynamic pricing system that adjusts the price of products in real-time based on factors like demand fluctuations, competition, inventory levels, and customer behavior. The AI models analyze vast amounts of historical and real-time data, allowing Zalando to optimize pricing in a way that benefits both the company and its customers.

- **Real-Time Price Adjustments**: The AI system considers factors such as demand trends, competitor prices, and stock availability to adjust prices dynamically. For instance, if a particular product becomes highly sought after, the AI will automatically increase the price, while in the case of slow-moving inventory, it will recommend discounts to stimulate sales.

- **Price Personalization**: Zalando's AI system also tailors prices based on customer segments, providing personalized pricing that enhances the shopping experience. For example, loyal customers might be offered discounts or exclusive pricing for certain products.

2.2 Challenges in Implementing AI in Dynamic Pricing:

- **Market Volatility**: Zalando must constantly adapt to market fluctuations. A sudden shift in demand, changes in competitor pricing, or external events (e.g., fashion trends, seasonality) can cause significant pricing volatility. The AI models must be agile and responsive enough to keep up with these dynamics.

- **Consumer Perception**: Dynamic pricing can sometimes lead to negative perceptions, as customers may feel frustrated by rapidly changing prices. If a customer purchases an item and sees the price drop shortly afterward, they may feel dissatisfied. Zalando works to balance AI-driven pricing adjustments with transparent and fair pricing strategies.

- **Data Accuracy**: For dynamic pricing to work effectively, the AI models must be fed accurate and up-to-date data. If data quality is compromised, pricing recommendations could be misleading, potentially leading to lost sales or unsatisfied customers.

2.3 Impact on Sales and Profitability:

Zalando's AI-driven pricing model has helped the company increase its revenue by ensuring that product prices are always optimized. This dynamic pricing approach allows Zalando to maintain competitive prices while maximizing margins during high-demand periods.

3. AI in Inventory and Supply Chain Management

3.1 Demand Forecasting with AI:

Zalando uses AI-powered tools for **demand forecasting** to predict customer purchasing behavior across different regions and segments. By analyzing historical sales data, seasonal trends, and external factors, the AI models provide highly accurate demand predictions for various products, allowing Zalando to plan inventory more efficiently.

- **Demand Prediction Models**: These models help Zalando predict how much of a particular product will be needed, both in specific markets and for specific customer segments. The AI takes into account trends in fashion, previous sales, and external factors like weather patterns or cultural events.

- **Stock Optimization**: With accurate demand forecasting, Zalando is able to stock the right amount of products at the right time, minimizing both overstock and stockouts. This reduces costs associated with storing excess inventory while ensuring popular products are always available for customers.

3.2 Automating Supply Chain Decisions Using AI:

10. AI for Customer Retention and Loyalty

AI has become a powerful tool in enhancing customer retention and loyalty, providing businesses with the ability to understand customer behavior more deeply. By analyzing vast amounts of data, AI can identify patterns in how customers interact with products and services.

This information allows companies to personalize their offerings, ensuring that each customer feels valued. For example, AI-driven algorithms can recommend products based on previous purchases or browsing history, making the shopping experience more tailored and engaging.

AI also helps in predicting future customer behavior. By utilizing predictive analytics, businesses can anticipate when a customer might be on the verge of leaving and take proactive steps to retain them. For instance, AI can detect a decline in a customer's engagement with the brand and trigger

- **Product Information Clarity:** Providing clearer, more accurate product descriptions and size information will help reduce misunderstandings and returns.

- **Feedback Loop Implementation:** The company should set up a system to continually gather and analyze customer feedback to monitor the effectiveness of the changes made.

In summary, using AI to analyze customer feedback provides actionable insights that can drive significant improvements in the customer experience, leading to better retention, increased satisfaction, and ultimately higher sales.

Zalando leverages AI for **supply chain automation**, where machine learning models analyze data in real time to make decisions about warehouse management, stock transfers, and fulfillment.

- **Optimized Warehousing**: The AI-driven system optimizes how products are stored in warehouses, ensuring that the most in-demand items are placed in the most accessible locations for quicker dispatch. It also automates restocking decisions to ensure a continuous supply of popular products.

- **Smart Logistics**: Zalando uses AI to predict the best logistics routes and methods for fulfilling customer orders. The AI system takes into account factors like delivery times, shipping costs, and real-time traffic data to ensure fast and cost-effective delivery.

3.3 AI for Inventory Replenishment and Stock Optimization:

Zalando uses AI to automatically replenish inventory based on the demand forecasts, ensuring that stock levels are optimized for each product. AI also helps manage stock turnover by recommending which products to restock first and which products to phase out based on sales data.

- **Predictive Replenishment**: The AI system ensures that popular products are always in stock by predicting which items need to be replenished and when. It also helps prevent overstocking by taking into account demand trends and sales velocity.

- **Supply Chain Visibility**: Zalando's AI-powered inventory system gives real-time visibility into stock levels, helping the company avoid disruptions in the supply chain and respond quickly to any unexpected demand surges.

4. Conclusion

Zalando's use of AI in **dynamic pricing**, **demand forecasting**, and **supply chain optimization** demonstrates the significant impact that AI can have on e-commerce operations. By using AI-powered systems to adjust prices in real-time, forecast demand, and optimize inventory, Zalando is able to provide a better customer experience, reduce operational costs, and increase profitability.

Despite challenges such as market volatility and data accuracy, Zalando's AI-driven approach has proven to be successful in enhancing its operational efficiency and maintaining competitiveness in the fast-paced fashion retail market. The company's integration of AI in its pricing and supply chain strategies offers valuable lessons for other e-commerce businesses seeking to harness the power of AI to drive growth and profitability.

13.7 Case Study 7: AI-Powered Visual Search for Product Discovery in E-Commerce - ASOS

1. Introduction

ASOS, a leading British online fashion and beauty retailer, has integrated **AI-powered visual search** into its platform to enhance the shopping experience for its millions of customers worldwide. This innovative AI technology allows customers to upload images or take photos of items they like, and the system will recommend similar products available on ASOS.

2. Visual Search and Image Recognition in E-Commerce

2.1 Role of AI in Visual Search:

Visual search technology, powered by artificial intelligence and computer vision, plays a central role in ASOS's strategy to provide a more intuitive and engaging shopping experience. It allows users to search for products by uploading images or using their smartphone camera to find similar items.

- **AI-Driven Product Discovery**: Instead of typing keywords or filtering through categories, customers can simply upload an image or take a photo of a product they want to find. The AI then analyzes the visual content and matches it with similar items in ASOS's product catalog, presenting a range of alternatives that are visually similar.

- **Enhanced Customer Experience**: Visual search technology makes it easier for customers to find what they are looking for, especially if they don't have the exact name or description of the item. It also helps customers discover items that they might not have thought to search for through traditional text-based searches.

2.2 Challenges in Implementing AI in Visual Search:

- **Image Quality and Variability**: A significant challenge in implementing visual search is ensuring that the AI can accurately interpret images taken in various environments, lighting conditions, or angles. For example, a customer may upload a blurry or poorly lit photo, which could make it difficult for the AI system to find the right matches.

- **Diverse Product Catalog**: ASOS offers millions of products across different categories and brands, so the AI system needs to handle a diverse range of clothing styles, colors, textures, and patterns. The complexity of matching visual similarities across such a large inventory can be a difficult task for AI.

- **User Experience**: For the AI-powered visual search to be truly effective, it needs to deliver highly relevant and accurate recommendations quickly. If the AI fails to produce useful results or takes too long to process, customers may lose interest or become frustrated.

2.3 Impact on Customer Engagement and Sales:

ASOS's visual search feature has led to increased engagement by making product discovery more seamless. Customers are more likely to stay engaged on the platform and continue browsing when they can quickly find similar items to those they are interested in. Additionally:

- **Increased Conversion Rates**: The ability to find exact matches or similar items based on an image increases the likelihood of a purchase. ASOS has reported higher conversion rates for users who engage with the visual search tool compared to those who only use text-based search.

- **Improved Customer Satisfaction**: By providing an innovative and user-friendly search experience, ASOS enhances customer satisfaction and loyalty. Visual search appeals to consumers who want a quick and efficient way to find products they like without having to navigate through numerous search filters.

3. Data Management Strategies for E-Commerce

3.1 Data Collection and Transformation:

ASOS collects large amounts of data to train its AI models for visual search. The company gathers product image data, customer interactions, and behavioral data to enhance the accuracy and relevance of the visual search recommendations.

- **Data Structuring**: The AI algorithms are trained on structured image data, which includes high-quality product photos, attributes such as color and pattern, and metadata like product descriptions and categories. ASOS continuously updates and curates this data to improve the AI model's performance.

- **Real-Time Data Processing**: The system uses real-time data to adapt to changing trends and customer preferences. This ensures that the visual search function remains relevant and up-to-date with current fashion trends, allowing the AI to recommend products that are in-demand at any given time.

3.2 Ensuring Data Privacy and Security:

ASOS is mindful of the privacy and security concerns related to the collection of user data. When customers upload photos for visual search, ASOS implements stringent security measures to protect sensitive information. Additionally, ASOS complies with data privacy regulations, including GDPR, to ensure that customer data is handled responsibly and transparently.

- **Data Minimization**: ASOS minimizes the amount of personal data collected during the visual search process, ensuring that only necessary image data is used for the AI's search capabilities.

- **Anonymization**: Personal data linked to the images, such as customer identifiers, is anonymized to protect user privacy. ASOS uses encrypted storage systems to ensure that all customer data is secure and cannot be accessed by unauthorized parties.

4. Conclusion

ASOS's adoption of **AI-powered visual search** for product discovery showcases the powerful potential of AI in enhancing the e-commerce shopping experience. By allowing customers to search for products based on images rather than text, ASOS has streamlined the process of discovering fashion items, which has led to improved engagement, higher conversion rates, and greater customer satisfaction.

Despite challenges related to image quality, diverse product offerings, and data privacy concerns, ASOS has successfully integrated visual search into its platform, setting a new standard for how e-commerce businesses can innovate using AI. This case study highlights the importance of effective data management, AI implementation, and user experience optimization for companies looking to enhance their e-commerce capabilities through advanced technologies.

www.ingramcontent.com/pod-product-compliance
Lightning Source LLC
LaVergne TN
LVHW081522050326
832903LV00025B/1593